Solo Parenting:
Raising Strong and Happy
Families

Solo Parenting

Diane Chambers

FAIRVIEW PRESS

Minneapolis

Published by Fairview Press, 2450 Riverside Avenue South, Minneapolis, MN 55454.

Library of Congress Cataloging-in-Publication Data

Chambers, Diane, 1960–
    Solo parenting : raising strong and happy families / by Diane Chambers.
        p.   cm.
    Includes bibliographical references
    ISBN 1-57749-008-8 (alk. paper)
    1. Single parents.   2. Single-parent family.   3. Parenting.   I. Title
    HQ759.915.C479   1997
    306.85'6—dc20
                                                            96-33586
                                                            CIP

First Printing: January 1997

Printed in the United States of America
01 00 99 98 97   7 6 5 4 3 2 1

Cover design: Circus Design
Author Photo: Jane Buss

Publisher's Note: Fairview Press publishes books and other materials related to the subjects of social and family issues. Its publications, including *Solo Parenting,* do not necessarily reflect the philosophy of Fairview Hospital and Healthcare Services or their treatment programs.

For a current catalog of Fairview Press titles, call toll-free 1-800-544-8207.

To Laura and Justin,
who provided daily inspiration.

CONTENTS

ACKNOWLEDGMENTS

I want to say "thanks" to the following individuals who have offered their experience or words of encouragement, or have been with me in spirit as I completed this project. To all of you, I'll be forever in debt.

To my loving husband, Bob Shearer. No other man could have held so steady through the roller coaster ride I experienced leading up to the completion of this book. Thank you for the endless hours you read, re-read, and edited the manuscript, and for offering honest opinions and loving criticism. I'll be forever in love with you and grateful for your true companionship.

To my parents, Bud and Ruth, who taught me important family values and provided that inherent "Chambers" fighting spirit.

To Mark Bacon, a good teacher, friend, and partner, who walked me through the tedious steps from idea to manuscript. Without your encouragement, I may not have continued toward the realization of my dream.

To the single parents who freely provided their personal stories, opening their hearts and lives to me without reservation: Julie Barber, Christopher Boyce, Teresa Burke, Sheri Fossett, Danita Gant, Chris Holder, Michelle Owens, Rebecca Stuck, and Vicky Wetenkamp.

To all those who assisted me with and participated in the initial single-parenting survey that got this project off the ground: Stella Collins, Karen Durst, Ruth Chambers, Ginny Jordano, Lucy DiChiara, Vicky Wetenkamp, Kim Chambers, Tina Chambers, Jodi Longenette, Sue Rickett, Jane Maalizadeh, Becky Taylor, Suzanne Hunt, Jan Williams, Julie Barber, Donna Husted,

Deborah Henighren, Linda Cochenour, Robyn Seitz, Sarah Galley, Vilma Escobar, Marie Cali, Nikki Harvey, Heather Stellabuto, Missy Steele, Karen Joslin, Kim Kiser, Lorri Yug, Liz Velasquez, Dana Rice, JoAnn Loewer, Lorraine Eastman, Deborah Anderson, Kelli Lamb, Sherena Landis, Elizabeth O'Ham, Tonya Kemp, Cathy Blazevich, Debbie Neber, Laura Hobbs, Terry Logan, Shari Mamone, Debbie Sproul, Jesselyn Laatz, Joan Gedde, Cindy Meyers, Amanda Dunkerly, Sonia Medrano, Paula Buffington, Janice Kasamis, Cindy Manouge, Cheri Pierce, Delores Broetzman, Betty Hamilin, John Pierce, and Terry Giffin.

To the Sole Mothers International Advisory Panel members who have offered their professional expertise whenever I needed guidance: Al Frankel, Patricia Larson, Robert Levy, Ed McClellan, Wendy McClelland, Jagdish Mehta, and Marlene Potter.

To special friends like Karen and Dave Durst, who put up with my late night phone calls when I was a struggling single parent; and to Vicky Wetenkamp for helping me keep life in perspective.

To my extended family members who were constantly cheering me on through word or spirit: Phyllis (Granny) Hanson, Don and Diane Chambers, Dave and Tina Chambers, Rob and Kim Chambers, Dan and Jodi Longenette, Andy Lloyd, Roy and Mary Chambers, Carmen and Mickey Cerreta (who purchased the first copy of my book long before I wrote it!), and to my beloved Aunt Phyllis Lloyd, who I wish could experience this with me (she's watching from afar).

Special thanks to Carolyn Hamilton-Proctor *(Nevada Woman)*, Mya Lake-Collins *(Las Vegas Kidz* magazine), and Mike Botula (Los Angeles County D.A.'s office) for helping me get my message out to single parents in need. Also special thanks to Dr. Don Moyer, Mary Hausch, and Ginny Jordano for always having an encouraging word.

Finally, a word of gratitude to my editors at Fairview Press, Julie Odland Smith and Lane Stiles, who treated me like a first class writer right from the beginning (when I didn't have a clue!).

Thanks, everyone, for your support of this project and continued support for Sole Mothers International.

INTRODUCTION

If we had no winter, spring would not be so pleasant; if we did not sometimes taste of adversity, prosperity would not be so welcome.
—Anne Bradstreet

One quarter of all American children will live in a single-parent family for at least some portion of their childhood. Many of these children, despite living in two separate households, will have healthy homes and the benefit of two loving parents. Others will experience successful blended families, and may even have the privilege of more than two loving caretakers influencing their lives. For those not so fortunate, however, the single-parent family will present a challenging, and often defeating, existence.

It is my hope that *Solo Parenting* will inspire single parents to take control of their own destinies through its proven step-by-step process. I believe all parents can overcome fate, environment, economic position, and past mistakes by making decisions motivated by love. This love must encompass our desire to give our children the best possible chances for success, and it requires the will to break unhealthy patterns. I believe nothing on this earth is stronger than parental love. And it is through that strength that single parents can achieve their dreams and provide a better world for their children.

Despite the disheartening statistics that reveal children of single-parent families are at risk, I stand firm in the belief that single parents can be effective and successful if they decide to be. In fact, during my research of this book, I encountered numerous single parents who professed to be better parents alone than many of their married counterparts are together. Although I maintain there is no better environment for a child than growing up in a well-balanced, two-parent household, I believe living with one healthy and mature parent is definitely better than existing in a combat zone with two childish ones. It may take more energy, more time, and more commitment to do it alone, but it can be done—and often in excellent style. I don't mean to suggest single parenting should be a coveted role, but merely one that should be viewed and approached with respect and pride. It's up to the millions of single parents out there in the present day to earn that respect by reaching for excellence and building confidence in their ability to raise healthy, responsible children. Take it from someone who knows: the sacrifices are well worth the rewards. In fact, the greater, and more painful, sacrifice is in the failure to attempt the journey toward successful single parenting, leaving our children's future to chance.

Most single parents can be categorized into four basic groups: single parents by unwanted pregnancy, single parents by divorce, single parents by deceased spouse, and single parents by choice. Each category comes with its own individual problems, circumstances, and nuances. It was unrealistic to think a guide could specifically address each of these situations in detail; therefore, this book takes into consideration the commonalities among the four groups and disregards how readers may have become single parents. In other words, regardless of how you acquired the role, the fact remains that you are raising a child or children on your own. I'm not interested in where you've been. I'm interested in where you're going. Being sensitive to this, I chose to draw on the kinship we feel with each other. This may leave a few unanswered questions for some of you, but the resource guide at the end of this book will give you information on how to find out more about specific issues not covered here.

I also had to recognize that single parenting crosses all social, economic, and racial boundaries. The emotional strength and fortitude necessary to succeed as a single parent, however, can't be bought, sold, or discriminated against. It is borne of a free will and a level of determination that is a part of the human spirit. Even so, I am sensitive to the differences in personality and circumstances that set me apart from the rest of my peers, recognizing that everyone brings unique experiences and social contexts to their single-parenting role. With these things in mind, I explored the common ground and approached each subject with care and practicality. Not surprisingly, after interviewing hundreds of single parents, I discovered enough common ground to write volumes of information.

I surveyed more than sixty people who were single parents, former single parents, or friends or family of single parents to discover what topics they wanted to see in a self-help book. These participants were from all over the country and ranged in age from twenty-two to fifty-four. Some were unemployed; others held professional positions. They unanimously agreed the top five subjects should be

1. Making career changes/Learning new skills
2. Budgeting/Living a good life on one income
3. Child-support issues
4. Child guidance/Disciplining on your own
5. Improving your children's chances for success in school and life

The chapters of this book follow their suggestions as well as my instincts. In addition, before writing this book I looked at the numerous parenting resource books on the market and tried to view them from the perspective of a single parent. I would open to the table of contents and find myself bombarded with a disjointed array of subjects: How to deal with finances, jobs, daycare, sassy children, your ex-husband's family, an unruly dog, even a bad hair day. Right away I felt overwhelmed and depressed that I might possibly be suffering in every one of these areas. Gasp! How would I begin to fix it all? These feelings helped me to see the need for a step-by-step format—something that followed a logical path of growth.

Solo Parenting gives you more than good advice on a variety of subjects. It gives you a road map to follow through the maze of single parenthood, with checkpoints now and then to make sure you're on the right track. The chapters follow a pattern consistent with the growth and emotional readiness experienced by most single parents. Part I will prepare you for the journey ahead with chapters on overcoming fear, reframing your situation, and turning negative emotions into positive steps. I believe this coincides with the initial days, weeks, and months of single parenthood. Part II concentrates on self-development by addressing career goals, financial concerns, and self-esteem, and naturally guides you on a path toward being better prepared to deal with parenting issues. Finally,

Part III will help you improve your child's chances of success by looking at discipline and responsibility, financial welfare, and reaching beyond the statistics toward a brighter future.

Before reading the first chapter, it is important to recognize a few basic principles about your single-parent experience.

- It's not going to go away (nor should that be your goal).
- Being a single parent is not synonymous with failure.
- Like it or not, your efforts (or lack thereof) will make a difference in other people's lives.
- Statistics show that you, and others like you, are literally raising the next generation.
- The dismal picture painted by statistics can be overcome.
- Happiness is not about finding a spouse or obtaining financial security. It's about learning contentment and finding joy in the life you have.

Although I am now happily remarried, I look back on my single-parent experience as the best years of my life—the years I learned what I was really made of. After moving in with my new husband, I decided to sell my former home. I'll never forget the tearful, bittersweet day I last visited it before the new owners moved in. Those walls had witnessed a lot of pain, but it had been a pain that had helped me to grow. The house was the only one I had ever owned all by myself. I remembered how hard I worked to make the monthly payments. I remembered the comforting smell of walking into it after a long day's work, kicking my shoes off and not caring where they landed. It was the domain my kids will always think of as Mom's place, where we laughed, talked, and shared stories. It was my haven of peace and quiet when the kids were visiting their father. It was the place where I stretched and struggled and grew.

As I walked from room to room that day, I realized that my second marriage was not a quick fix for loneliness or a way to say good-bye to the past. It was a new and separate chapter in my life, set apart from my years as a single parent. I wasn't saying good-bye, I was merely folding up that part of my life and laying it tenderly in the memory trunk to return to on occasion as one returns to a treasured family heirloom. Those years will always mean a lot to me. After all, it was during those years that my journey toward self-discovery began—a journey that ultimately propelled me into a wonderful future with a caring partner and a strong sense of self-worth. I can't say good-bye to what I learned just because I am no longer parenting alone. In the following pages I share with you some of the rich experiences that you can look forward to as a successful single parent.

PART ONE:

Preparation

1

Overcoming Fear

Nothing in life is to be feared. It is only to be understood.

—Marie Curie

A Journey to Freedom

Facing the prospects of divorce and single motherhood were the least of Julie's fears. Dealing with the typical concerns about making ends meet or raising a child alone had to take a back seat to the realities of her physically abusive marriage. Her first priority was to figure out how to escape from her situation alive. Julie had two choices: Stay and continually subject herself and her three-year-old daughter Cherish to violence and pain, or leave and take the chance that her husband's threats to kill her if she did was more than just wild talk. Julie looked at her possibilities, mustered up her courage, and chose to leave.

"I guess one day, after one of his episodes, I realized I was going to die, literally, in this marriage," Julie recounts. "Then I wondered what would happen to my daughter and how he might begin to hurt her as she got older. Even though he threatened to kill me if I left, I knew my chances of dying were greater if I stayed. So I took the risk."

Julie's story began when she was only fourteen. She met her future husband at a Halloween party and fell in love. "He was six-foot-six and so good-looking. When we started dating a couple of years later, all my friends were so envious of me. I was sure it was the beginning of a wonderful life."

The abuse, mostly verbal at first, began shortly after they moved in together. "It was always after he had been drinking," Julie says. "So I just thought it was the alcohol talking, not him."

As the years went on, the abuse became increasingly physical until Julie discovered she was pregnant with their first child. "Most men become more abusive to their pregnant wives, but my husband really mellowed during that time. He was happy about the baby coming and he helped me a lot with her after she was born. I really thought he was finally growing up and the nightmare was over."

It wasn't long before Julie's husband began drinking and abusing her again. "He was a total Jekyll and Hyde. As a drunk, he was mean, but when he was sober, he was totally opposite. He would kiss the ground I walked on sometimes and could be so sweet. I was convinced it was the alcohol. We tried AA meetings but he could never admit his problem. I called the police a number of times and he actually was arrested once. I couldn't understand why I always had to leave, though, but restraining orders against him were only temporary. Counseling didn't work because he said the counselors were just trying to break us up.

"It got to the point he had full control of everything I did. I started going to the shelters and they would tell me I had to leave him. But I couldn't figure out how, because he made sure I wasn't working and didn't have any way out. I felt trapped."

Julie was a prisoner in her own home. The longer she stayed with him, the more her personal freedom dwindled.

"I couldn't go to the grocery store without coming home to accusations and abuse. One time I tried to defend myself after he kicked me all the way to the bathroom. I got up and really let him have it, but it was the worst mistake I ever made. I got it twice as bad after that. The next day after seeing my black eye, he broke down and cried and said he'd never do it again. When you see a grown man cry—someone you love—it makes it that much harder to leave. I wanted to make it work in the worst way."

Fear for her life drove Julie away night after night as she desperately tried to run from the problem. She attempted to leave her husband on more than twenty different occasions, finding refuge in nearby Las Vegas hotels, shelters, friends' homes . . . anywhere to get away.

"I ran up my credit card bills at the hotels because I would have to leave in the middle of the night. I would get Cherish out of bed and just leave because I was so scared. When I couldn't afford the hotels any longer, we would just find a place to park and sleep in the car. I would cry all night long about it, but at least I felt safe."

"Julie, just leave him. Please go," her friends would plead in frustration, but she just didn't see a way out. Eventually, she began having fantasies of killing her husband. "I rationalized my thoughts. It was either going to be me or him. I knew then I had gone over the edge."

She said her husband laughed at her accusations and ridiculed her fears, always telling her she was overreacting. "I started thinking I was the one who was crazy," she says. He put on a completely different face in front of his friends and family. None of them could believe he would do anything to hurt me. But I knew."

After five years of abuse, Julie began daydreaming of freedom. She started looking in the want ads for jobs, apartments, anything that might be her ticket to a new life.

"I really didn't think I'd have the courage to do it, but I looked anyway, just in case. One day I saw an ad about a single mom wanting to rent out a room in her home. I contacted her and we started to develop a friendship. She told me about a pro bono program that could help me get a low-cost divorce, and she offered her master bedroom and bath to me and Cherish.

"Around the same time, I saw an ad in the paper for a part-time job at a local bank. My husband reluctantly agreed to let me apply for the job. Then I secretly started saving my nest egg. I was on my way."

With the help of another single mother and the part-time job at the bank, Julie found the courage to break away from her abusive situation. "With a pounding heart and fear for my life, I left him. The day he was served divorce papers he called and said he was going to kill me. He said if he ever saw me and my daughter in the car he would run us off the road and kill us. I ran in fear for about six months after that, until he met someone else to abuse. Then he left us alone."

Julie now works full-time as a collections representative and lives with her daughter in a two-bedroom apartment. She says her next goal is to save enough money for a down payment on a home of her own.

"So many times I've thought, 'How did you do it, Julie? How did you survive?' I didn't think I'd ever get out of that mess alive. But wanting to protect my daughter gave me the determination to do it. Now we're a thriving single-parent family with a lot to look forward to."

Julie's advice to single parents is this: "Whatever your fear, don't try to tackle it alone. There's always someone who is willing to help you. Don't let pride or humiliation get in the way. You can do it."

❊❊❊❊❊❊❊❊

When Julie told me her story, I almost felt ashamed of the trivial fears I had experienced going into single parenthood. I can thankfully say I never feared for my life or the lives of my children. Regardless, the anxiety I felt as I faced single parenthood was real and it hurt. No one is exempt from fear—it's a natural human response to the threat of change. Nor is single parenting unique to any certain group of people, making us all vulnerable to the uncertainties that accompany the role. Shoshana Alexander put it well in her book *In Praise of Single Parents:*

> We are from all socioeconomic classes, from every ethnic group, every
> profession, every sexual orientation. Welfare recipients and film stars are
> single parents. Whoever we are, raising our children on our own may be
> both one of the most rewarding tasks of our lives and one of the hardest we ever undertake.[1]

Don't feel guilty or inadequate because you are afraid, even if your fear seems unfounded to family and friends. No matter what the circumstances, fear can and will paralyze you if you allow it to control your decisions. The first step in overcoming fear, then, is to accept it as a normal condition of the single-parenting experience.

Franklin Delano Roosevelt said that "the only thing we have to fear is fear itself." As wise as Roosevelt's observation was, his wife Eleanor offered even more wisdom when she said, "I believe that anyone can conquer fear by doing the things he fears to do, provided he keeps doing them until he gets a record of successful experiences behind him." Successful experiences are something we all covet, and with every one we become more and more confident in our ability to face another challenge. My first attempt to conquer fear occurred when I was about ten years old. I had a phobia of high places, and I tried to conquer it by jumping off the high dive with my friends at our community swimming pool. I was determined to do it, mainly because I didn't want to look like a chicken in front of my friends. As I walked up the ladder (which was all of ten feet), it seemed as if I were climbing a mountain. My palms sweated, I felt dizzy. I knew the moment of truth had come. I couldn't turn around and go back; I had to do it. I didn't dive gracefully like a pro. I didn't even bend the board. I walked to the end of the board with my eyes straight ahead. I held my nose, closed my eyes tight, and stepped slowly off. After a fall that seemed like an eternity, I hit the water, quickly came to the surface, and swam to the edge with a big smile on my face. I had done it!

I never did completely overcome my fear of heights. To this day, my kids tease me because I can't look out a second-story window without getting sweaty palms. However, because I had a few successful experiences that didn't result in death or harm, I felt more confident about the outcome each time I made an attempt to jump. I learned I was capable of facing my fear and accomplishing my goal, in spite of my pounding heart. The successful experiences Eleanor Roosevelt spoke of can only come through repeated, courageous attempts to face our fears head-on.

Since single parenthood rarely begins under pleasant circumstances, it's easy to look at the unsuccessful experiences in your life and use them as a point of reference for the future—hence, the birth of fear. "What ifs" begin to creep in. "What if I can't make it financially?" "What if I can't control my children?" "What if I lose custody?" "What if I can't be intimate with anyone again?" "What if?" "What if?"

From my research for this book, I learned that the most common fears single parents face can be grouped into three categories:

- Financial

  Losing employment or housing

  Inability to pay utility bills, buy food or clothing, and so on

- Parenting
    Losing control (especially with older children)
    Losing custody
    Inability to expend the energy and time needed to be an effective parent
    Inability to provide a healthy environment
- Personal
    Being alone
    Inability to establish meaningful relationships
    Dating and how it might affect children
    Failure in career or personal goals

It's easy to see why someone entering the world of single parenting might have a lot of questions about his or her future. Although most optimists will steer you away from asking all the "what ifs," I'm going to encourage it, simply because it helps you pinpoint the root cause of your fear. "What if I jump off the high dive and discover all the water has been drained from the pool?" "What if I have a heart attack on the way down?" "What if they laugh at me for looking scared to death?" When I put my fear into perspective, I discovered I had no real foundation to base my anxiety on other than silly misconceptions. Nine times out of ten, the answers are simple and obvious. But for the 10 percent that still leave you hanging, the following five-step process will help you turn fear into action.

"If I Can't Get Rid of It, What Do I Do with It?"

Shortly after my divorce, I began a long streak of sleepless nights. I regularly tossed and turned with anxiety about my future. One night, as I was overwhelmed by insomnia, I began to analyze the reasons behind my sleeplessness. I quickly discovered a common thread. Night after night, I was continually rehashing the same problems and concerns. Making a mental list was only perpetuating my sleep disorder. That's when I came up with the idea of keeping a bedside notebook. I made a written list of the things that were bothering me. This is how I began:

My expenses exceed my income. How will I ever pay the bills?
I'm an emotional wreck. How can I possibly be a good mother?
My car is on its last leg. What if it breaks down?

I haven't dated in years. What if someone asks me out?

My ex-husband is unpredictable. What if he can't pay child support or wants more visitation rights?

I wrote down my concerns and followed each with a hypothetical question. Then I ranked them in order of intensity. At first it was difficult because it seemed they all were intense and critical. I zeroed in on the number one fear, which happened to be the first on my list. How will I ever pay the bills? I temporarily put aside, at least for the night, the rest of my concerns and looked at only this issue. Then I went through a series of questions. Why were my expenses so high? I concluded I had too much debt. The divorce had forced me to split outstanding debts with my ex-husband, leaving me with more expenses than income. I then asked myself what was different between now and before I became a single parent. My ex-husband and I always had debt to pay, but somehow knowing there was another person sharing the problem made it easier. Aha! I didn't fear the debt as much as I feared facing it alone. The next logical step was to write down the name of someone who could help.

My boss: could give me a raise (dream on)

My parents: could loan me the money (nah!)

Creditors: could work out new repayment plan (hmmm . . .)

Consumer credit counseling: I read somewhere they offer free advice (that's it!)

Without much contemplation, I quickly ruled out the first two possibilities, but decided I could probably handle the last two. After I made the decision to contact someone the next day, I went to sleep knowing I had a plan.

I didn't try to solve my financial dilemma that night. I just made one simple decision to involve someone else. Two heads really are better than one, so don't let pride get in the way of a good night's sleep. When Julie made the decision to break away from her husband, she garnered the support of her friends and family, but more importantly, she acted upon her fear by talking to someone about a part-time job. Her courage manifested itself through her action.

Step #1
Get it on paper.

- Pinpoint the root cause of your fear.
- List names of people who can help.
- Discuss possible solutions with them.

The Short-Term Solution

You will find that most fears are easily put to rest by looking at the "what if" questions realistically. Sometimes it takes a friend or professional to help you see there is really nothing to be concerned about. However, as I stated before, there will be some fears on your list that warrant concern and action. The best way to handle those fears is to devise a plan to deal with them. My fear of the debt I owed was a legitimate concern. Writing it down and recording the name of someone who could help turned the fear into a manageable problem. The next step was to work through the possible solutions with helpful counsel. In my case, working with creditors on an easier repayment schedule and eventually working toward making more money were good plans. The short-term plan should be financially and emotionally manageable and should relieve the symptoms of the problem or fear. Let's look at another example.

Karen's number one fear is not being able to find adequate daycare for her children. Before becoming a single mom, her household income allowed her to afford the best daycare centers. Now, she can barely afford the least expensive care. Remember, the first rule is to write it down: pinpoint the root cause and list those who can help. Karen's short-term decision may involve an immediate change in her daycare situation or possibly job rescheduling. In the long term, changing jobs or finding ways to make more money might be her goals. People who can help might be her family members, friends, or a daycare referral service.

Karen commits to talking to at least three people about her situation before making a decision. After discussing things with them, she makes a list of all possible choices, preferably with pros and cons next to each one. From her list, she uses the process of elimination to find the choice she feels most comfortable with. Now she's ready to take the action necessary to relieve the symptoms of the problem. Her last step is to write down a long-term goal that will keep her from having to deal with this same fear again in the future. Karen can sleep easier knowing she has taken a proactive approach to her fear.

Step #2
Turn legitimate fear into
manageable problems.

- Write down all possible choices.
- Choose a manageable short-term solution.
- Devise a long-term plan to prevent future problems.

The Long-Term Goals

Once short-term fears are dispelled, you may still be left with fear of encountering some of the same problems in the future. This is the purpose of devising a long-term plan. Working toward long-term goals such as changing careers or becoming a more effective parent can be an overwhelming prospect.

Dr. Thomas Whiteman, in his Fresh Start program for single parents, says, "Every journey starts with a single step—and it continues with a series of single steps."[2] Before rushing into action (which will be discussed further in chapter 3), though, it's important to gather information about your journey. When you're trying to work through the fear, you simply are not yet ready to take action. However, gathering information will help you to become increasingly comfortable with the prospect of setting out on a new and different journey. You wouldn't normally take off on a vacation without knowing where you were going, how you were going to get there, where you were going to stay, and how much you were going to have to pay. In the same way, simply making a choice or setting a goal doesn't solve a problem. Neither does starting a journey you know nothing about. It is important to make the change a lasting one by gathering information and becoming knowledgeable about the journey you're considering.

The process of informing yourself is fairly simple and noncommittal. By making phone calls, writing letters, reading articles and books, and talking with the right people, you can build your confidence about the decision. Get to know your way around the local library. It's a great place to hang out, for both you and your kids. It's educational, informative, and surprisingly fun. When I started looking for ways to entertain my kids after I became a single mom, the library was one of the first places I found to be a quiet and fun refuge for us all. Many times I would browse around, not looking for any particular type of information. I would always pick up something of use, such as books full of tips on how to clean my house more efficiently, take a low-budget vacation, or care for a hamster (of which we had many). Going to the library is also an effective way to instill a love of books and knowledge in your kids.

Once you are familiar with the type of information you need, you can take these few steps to make the decision-making process a little easier:

- First, start a file on the subject you're investigating (college, law, finances, and so on). As you gather information, file it away until you're ready to make the journey. You will feel so much better about making a decision based on all the information you've collected over an extended period of time.

- Second, get to know the reference librarian at your community library. His or her job is to help you find the information you need, so your research need not become a frustrating experience. The librarian can help you learn how to use the library's catalog system (most are computerized now) and can direct you to mounds of information on nearly any subject you might be interested in.

- Third, keep your eyes and ears open for information wherever you go. Grocery stores, department stores, and other public locations generally provide racks with free pamphlets, magazines, and periodicals that have a variety of information to offer. Don't be afraid to visit local government buildings, including colleges and universities, where you might pick up information on family-counseling programs, parenting seminars, educational opportunities, and much more.

These are all places where the general public is usually welcome and where it is not out of line to approach a receptionist or clerk to ask for help. Most of the time, you will find people are willing to help and appreciate your interest. If they aren't, keep asking until you find someone who is. Your persistence will pay off ten-fold down the road. You'll soon discover finding information is not difficult at all. The real problem is in finding the time to sift through it all. If you commit to adding something to your file every week, you will be surprised at your rich supply when you are mentally ready to embark on the journey.

One reason gathering information is so important in the beginning is that it helps to keep your spirits up and to remind you that you are doing something to improve your future. Don't rush going from the idea stage to the action stage. Allow yourself ample time to look at all possibilities, and have fun doing it. For example: Maybe you've decided you might like to go back to college one day so that you can have a career that will provide the lifestyle you want for your children. You're afraid of the sacrifices that might cause other problems in your already complicated life, and the thought of returning to school and taking tests causes you to break out in a cold sweat. Is the answer to start taking night classes right away? Not necessarily.

When I decided to pursue a college degree, I was terrified. I had only taken one college course in my lifetime and that was when I was eighteen years old. I didn't know what I would encounter or if I would have what was needed to succeed. I visited the local community college on my lunch hour one day just to get a sense of what to expect. I didn't talk to anyone, and I didn't pick up any information; I just walked around. I left after about twenty minutes. It was scary.

About a week later, I made a phone call to one of the counselors to get more information. She sent me a packet, and I spent a few weeks looking it over. Each time I looked at it, I would get a sick feeling in my stomach. I knew I wanted to do it, but it was all so new to me. I discovered there was an orientation seminar for new students, and I attended one evening after work. Again, I took the information home and spent a few weeks "looking it over." Eventually, when it came time to register for classes, I had a good idea of what it was all about. I had talked to the right people, I had visited the campus on a few occasions, and I had gotten enough information to make the right decisions. Knowing what to do to get started helped me to be less fearful about the experience. I took one small step, followed by a series of more small steps. I'm now a college graduate and it seems like only yesterday I was doubting my ability to take even one class. Knowledge is power when it comes to overcoming fear. Start early and take your time getting to know all the facts.

Step #3
Inform yourself.

- Make phone calls, write letters, read books and articles.
- Start a file; add to it on a regular basis.
- Always keep your eyes and ears open for new information.

Acceptance Will Set You Free

More often than not, the things we fear most are those we have the least control over. There's a logical reason for this. If we think we can change our situation, we feel more in control and tend to have less fear of the outcome. When I looked over my original list of fears, the second most intense situation was the unpredictability of my ex-husband. I feared his actions because they could affect my financial well-being as well as my relationship with my kids. I worried about this daily until I found a little coin with an old but wise saying on it. A good friend had given it to me several years before when I was going through some personal problems. It said, "God grant me the serenity to accept the things I cannot change, the courage to change the things I can, and the wisdom to know the difference.

I began applying this rule whenever a new fear would creep up on me. I knew my ex-husband's unpredictability was out of my control. I couldn't solve that dilemma, so it was useless to worry about it. I took action in the areas in which I had control by getting a court order for child support and visitation, but I stopped worrying about the rest. I made a promise to myself to concentrate only on those things I could control and deal with any uncontrollable circumstances as they arose. For the out-of-your-control fears on your list, make a little note to yourself that reads, "I can't control this outcome," then try to forget about it.

One of the toughest lessons life teaches us is acceptance. It's like trying to swallow a huge pill that you just can't seem to get down. For many of us, it's a struggle to admit to ourselves that life is not perfect, no matter how hard we try to make it so. I remember hating the thought of being part of the divorce statistics. Divorce meant failure. Single motherhood meant weakness. Broken families meant trouble. I didn't want to be part of any of it, so I tried to pretend I wasn't for a while. Sooner or later, though, I had to come to grips with being one of "them." And when I did, something wonderful happened: I was freed from the notion that I had to be perfect. That was the beginning of true liberation for me. Until Julie started talking to others about it, she probably thought that she had to accept her abusive situation. Eventually she discovered she had more control than she thought. In her situation, it was simply a matter of knowing the difference.

Step #4
Accept what you cannot change.

- Quickly dispel fear of circumstances that are out of your control.
- Concentrate only on problems you can control.
- Seek spiritual guidance to know the difference.

Count Your Blessings

"There's always someone worse off than you," my grandmother would say about my trivial childhood complaints. I didn't like hearing that, although it was undeniably true. "Is that supposed to make me feel better?" I thought. In a way, it caused me to feel insignificant, and as a youngster growing up, I wanted to feel significant. As I grew older, however, and experienced more pain, I found myself striving for the positive. I didn't want to stand out in a negative way; I wanted people to notice a positive significance in my life. In order for others to notice, I had to first recognize it in myself.

In the same way, single parents are highly susceptible to the "woe is me" syndrome because of the enormous amount of responsibility and uncertainty they often face. Consequently, fear overtakes us when we don't know what to expect or haven't planned ahead. After pinpointing the causes of our fears, talking with someone about them, devising short- and long-term plans, and accepting the things we cannot change, the last step in strengthening our resistance to fear is discovering the positives in our lives and building ourselves up. Let's go back and look at my original list of fears:

1. My expenses exceed my income. How will I ever pay the bills?
2. I'm an emotional wreck. How can I possibly be a good mother?
3. My car is on its last leg. What if it breaks down?
4. I haven't dated in years. What if someone asks me out?
5. My ex-husband is unpredictable. What if he can't pay child support or wants more visitation rights?

If I take each concern and come up with an alternate positive, or "safety feature," as I like to call it, this is what I get:

1. I'm thankful I have a job. I also have the ability to work through my financial problems.
2. My emotional turmoil is only temporary. Millions of women have experienced divorce and are great mothers, raising happy, responsible children.
3. I have lots of friends and family members who would help me get my car in shape. All I need to do is ask.
4. I'll feel flattered if someone asks me out. That must mean I'm attractive and someone might enjoy my company. I won't go if I don't want to.
5. He is paying child support now and spends time with the kids. My children need to know their father and spend time with him on a regular basis.

Something positive can usually be found in every negative situation. Learn to look at the good in your life. You might surprise yourself with how much you have going for you instead of against you. Negative things rarely "happen" to us; more often, we set the stage by allowing our fears to wear us down, making us magnets to all the negative particles floating around.

Step #5
Discover the good in your life.

- Find a positive in every negative.
- Write down "safety features" of every fear.
- When fear begins to overwhelm you, think positive.

In a Nutshell

"Life is difficult," Dr. M. Scott Peck writes in his bestseller *The Road Less Traveled.* "What makes life difficult is that the process of confronting and solving problems is a painful one. Yet it is in the whole process of meeting and solving problems that life has its meaning. Problems are the cutting edge that distinguishes between success and failure. Problems call forth our courage and our wisdom."[3]

Life-changing experiences, such as the one that probably introduced you to single parenthood, naturally cause a certain amount of fear and uncertainty. Fear is a natural human response designed to get our hearts pounding a little harder, our adrenaline flowing a little faster, our minds thinking more clearly and sharply than when we're relaxed and sedate. To paraphrase Franklin Roosevelt, fearing the emotion only paralyzes us and keeps us from responding wisely.

A wise way to handle fear is to see it as a means to an end. You may feel immobile at first, but use your instincts and enlist the help of others to take small steps toward familiarizing yourself with your new role as a single parent. The five steps outlined above to help you overcome fear will not solve your problems; ultimately, you must take some sort of action to do that. But getting in touch with your fears, accepting what you cannot change, and looking in a positive direction is a great place to start.

Checkpoint

- Have you written all your fears on paper?
- Are you building a list of people who can help?
- Have you devised a short-term plan?
- Have you written down some long-term goals?
- Are you gathering information for the journey?
- Have you put aside what you cannot change?
- Have you listed positives for every fear?
- Are you feeling more confident than before?

If you can answer yes to all these questions, go on to chapter 2.

2

REFRAMING

Life is under no obligation to give us what we expect.

—Margaret Mitchell

From Fairy Tale to Reality

Carol knew her marriage to Dan was coming to an end when she first discovered he was having an affair. Pregnant with their third child, Carol thought it couldn't be happening to her. Much to her surprise and dismay, everything became painfully real at her moment of truth.

"We had been trying to have a baby . . . or I guess you could say *I* was trying," Carol said. "Little did I know he was already into the affair when I told him I was pregnant. He became enraged. It really hurt. He stopped paying attention to me at that point—as if I had thrown a monkey wrench into his plans.

"Our sex life came to a halt in my fifth month of pregnancy. I started sleeping in the other room, but it was fine because at least we weren't fighting anymore. I remember telling a friend that our marriage was improving," she said with a laugh. "I told her we used to fight all the time, but things had calmed down. I didn't know it then, but he seemed happy because he was in love with someone else.

"I remember waiting until he was asleep, and then I'd go out into the living room and sit in a chair crying. One night he heard me and came out to see what was wrong. I asked him, 'Why won't you touch me anymore?' Of course, I thought it was because I had gained weight and just wasn't desirable to him. He said, 'I don't know. I haven't been taking good care of you lately. I promise I'll start taking care of you.' He promised, and I believed him."

She began noticing changes in Dan's routine shortly after the birth of the baby. Carol said she felt he was either having an affair or the strain of having a new baby was making her crazy.

"He started going out one night a week, supposedly with the guys, but since he never did that before, I really thought it was odd. It wasn't long before I started noticing telltale signs like makeup on his collar and the smell of a woman's perfume on his shirt. It got to the point where I couldn't sleep next to him anymore. I just got this really awful feeling."

When she confronted Dan about her suspicion, he denied it vehemently, telling her how much he loved her. "He was playing with my mind," Carol remembers. "My self-esteem was already pretty low, and he knew how to make it even worse. Eventually, I had to find out just so I would know I wasn't crazy like he insisted I was."

She felt like she was betraying her husband because she didn't believe him. Carol also found it difficult to talk to her family and friends because it was too humiliating to admit her marriage had taken a turn for the worse. She finally got the courage to contact someone with a more objective point of view who could help. Contrary to everything she had been raised to believe, or wanted to believe, she put marital trust aside and hired a private detective to discover the truth. It was then that Carol's suspicions became reality.

"Even though I knew something was up, I was still in shock when the detective confirmed I was right. I'll never forget the night he called me from a local bar to tell me my husband was there slobbering all over another woman. My body went numb, completely numb."

Once her suspicions about Dan were verified, Carol knew things would never be the way they used to be. Feelings of betrayal, mistrust, and disappointment flooded her heart. "How could he do this now?" she repeatedly asked herself. "Especially now."

"After twelve years of marriage, there was nothing left but the three children we shared and a lot of broken promises," Carol recounts. "The fear and uncertainty I faced as a single mom were overwhelming. I didn't know how I was going to make it through."

A strict Baptist upbringing made it even tougher for Carol to accept her fate. Like millions of other women in her position, she was overcome with guilt, wondering why she was not able to prevent this from happening in her life. She considered herself a good Christian, a loving mother, and a devoted wife. Carol initially blamed herself for the breakup and found it impossible to view the situation positively, even though she felt her anger was morally justified.

"Right away, I wondered what I did wrong. Maybe if I had loved him better, did this or that different, maybe it wouldn't have happened. I went to our church pastor for counseling and told him, 'I can't get a divorce.' He responded in an understanding tone, 'Yes you can. Your husband was unfaithful.' I thought to myself, 'No I can't. Dan is my security. I have a brand new baby plus two other children to support. What's going to happen to my house, where will we live?'

"I confronted Dan about the affair, hoping he would want to give up the girl and save his family. I convinced him to go to counseling with me, but he continued to see her. Finally, I gave him an ultimatum. I couldn't live with a girlfriend in the picture.

"He continued to deny it, and for a while, I questioned myself. But there were pictures to prove it. He just said it wasn't what I thought; they were just friends. He called me a liar and a traitor. He said he would make the rest of my life a living hell, and he did a pretty good job of it. It hurt and I was scared."

It was several months before Carol's nightmare came to a halt. Once the divorce was over, she began to regain her self-respect, but it took a series of successes. "I remember feeling self-conscious about being divorced," she says, "especially in church. I was afraid some of my old friends wouldn't want to be around me anymore. In fact, some of them did pull away because they were married and didn't want to catch 'divorce fever.' I went through a transformation during this time. I began looking deeper inside myself and asking simple questions: 'How did I get here? What did I do wrong? How can I prevent making these same mistakes again?' Eventually I reconciled things and realized the trials were necessary to my ultimate growth. I wouldn't give up who I am now for the world."

Carol's faith came back in new ways. She said she began looking at the whole picture in a brand new light. "Getting married the first time just seemed like the right thing to do for me then. I'm not even sure we truly loved each other. We were so young. I had no idea what it would take to keep a relationship going.

"Now I say prayers of thanks for the peace in my life. I am very thankful to look back and say, 'I don't have to live like that anymore.' I had been living a lie, and now I can finally be true to myself and my beliefs."

Carol says the change didn't come overnight. Gradually she began to see God as her new husband and provider. "Together, he and I became a pretty good team."

After a painful divorce, Carol said her grieving led to a new pattern of decision-making. "I had spent so much time doing what everyone told me to do, I failed to ever ask what I wanted for me," she said. "Now I spend more time listening to my heart for answers, and I put less weight on what others tell me. Now that I know myself better, and what I want out of life, it's much easier to look to the future with confidence."

❖❖❖❖❖❖❖❖❖

Grief is a feeling that some people associate only with the death of a loved one, but, in fact, it is an emotion shared by many single parents like Carol who have lost a partner through adultery. Even single parents who never married or never lived with the other parent may grieve over the loss of a particular lifestyle or relationship that might have been. Consequently, most single parents should expect to work through the grief process, allowing themselves to experience denial, anger, depression, and acceptance.

Fear, as we discussed in chapter 1, is only one of the obstacles associated with facing the single-parent lifestyle. In order to take steps toward success, it is also necessary to come to a healthy conclusion about your new role. This will require learning to look at yourself and the world in a new light by channeling the grief or loss in a positive manner. This is one of the toughest steps you'll take, and is one that requires ongoing attention. A veteran single mom who has been managing her family successfully for years will still have occasional bouts of depression or self-doubt simply because of the tremendous responsibility she faces alone. However, the goal is to learn to deal with these feelings in a positive way so that they recur less frequently and with less intensity.

Old Picture, New Frame

The idea of reframing was first introduced to me a couple of years ago in a communication theory course. According to Paul Watzlawick, a well-known researcher in the field of communications, to "reframe" is "to change the conceptual and/or emotional setting or viewpoint in relation to which a situation is experienced and to place it in another frame which fits the "facts" of the same concrete situation equally well or even better, and thereby changes its entire meaning."[1]

To make the definition a little more understandable to the reader, Watzlawick relates a story about a man with a bad stammer who, for reasons unknown, had no other alternative but to try his luck as a salesman. His employer was apprehensive at first, but felt sorry for him and decided to let him give it a try. Curiously enough, the man did exceptionally well on his first attempts. Because salesmen are generally disliked for their slick way of talking, the man was appealing to many people because the usual stereotypes didn't apply in his case. In fact, customers listened carefully and patiently to his convincing message. He was so successful that his boss instructed him to continue his stammering even if he began to feel more at ease. What was once thought of as the man's handicap became his greatest asset on the job.

Reframing a situation is difficult because we tend to categorize everything as either good or bad, Watzlawick says, based on our experiences of the world. And once we've categorized something, we have a hard time seeing it in any other light. Our perception becomes our reality. We see our viewpoint as good, and we see other people's viewpoints as bad.

If you were raised in a religious home, you were probably taught that being divorced or having a child out of wedlock was bad. Having been raised in a traditional home on a Midwest farm, I viewed divorce as something foreign to my existence. I knew it was out there, but I never thought I would experience it. Likewise, new single parents often have negative thoughts about their situations., seeing them as

- temporary ("I hope a partner will come along to make it go away.")
- incomplete ("I'm only half as good without my other half.")
- inferior ("My family is not as respectable as a two-parent family.")
- punitive ("I deserve this pain.")

Rarely do they see their families in a positive light, as, for example,

- lasting ("My kids will always remember my dedication.")
- complete ("We have a special bond.")
- superior ("My kids are learning to be responsible.")
- privileged ("I—and not my ex—get all the rewards!")

In order to get from the negative thoughts to the positive ones, a period of reframing must take place. This can take a couple of months, or years, depending on how motivated and receptive you are to the idea. Fortunately, Watzlawick says once we are able to come through the reframing process, it's nearly impossible to go back to our old way of thinking. It's similar to when you first discover there is no Santa Claus. Initially, it's a shock and you feel let down because you want so badly to believe that he exists. But once you are able to reframe and see the Christmas season in a new light, you discover the wonderful and selfless gift of giving, and it's impossible to return to your former, more selfish, way of viewing the holiday.

To better understand this concept of reframing, let's look at another example, this one from a child's point of view. When my son Justin was ten years old, he began showing signs of nearsightedness and refused to admit he was having trouble seeing far away. When I would question him about this, he would become angry and say, "Mom, I don't need glasses, okay?" When his teacher mentioned it to me, I knew I wasn't imagining things, so I made an appointment with the optometrist. Justin worried for days about the appointment because he didn't want to face the inevitable: he was going to have to wear eyeglasses. All he could think about was the other kids in his class making fun of him and calling him "four eyes." When the expected news came that he indeed needed the dreaded spectacles, I tried to soften the blow by letting him pick out some really "cool" frames that might make him feel a little better about himself.

To make a long story short, he came home a few days later with the news that he had a secret admirer at school. He beamed when he talked about the anonymous note he found on his desk that read, "I really like you in your new glasses. From a secret admirer." Boy, did his attitude change! Justin's situation had literally been reframed: he discovered that life was actually better after eye-glasses. Not only could he see more clearly, he learned that what may seem like a negative can often turn out to be a positive.

Suddenly becoming single after spending several years with a partner can be a frightening experience. Those who lose their mates to death or adultery usually have the toughest time reframing their broken family portrait. Most often, these parents are forced into a new lifestyle before they've had a chance to make any choices for themselves. What's more, their pain tends to magnify the situation as they struggle to put aside the love they still feel for their deceased spouse, or even their estranged partner.

Here is a three-step process to help you work through some of these feelings so that you can begin to reframe your own situation.

Letting Go of the Way Things Used to Be

When we're hurting, it's natural to want to place blame somewhere. We often become enraged when we think about all the things we used to have before our lives were interrupted by death, divorce, or unwanted pregnancy. We end up blaming God or our ex-partners for our current situation and have a tough time accepting things as they are. It's easy at this point to idealize the past, but don't get caught up in selective memory.

I often think about my childhood, and how much simpler life on the mid-western farm was compared to the hustle and bustle of the city where I now live. I always think about the wonderful smell that wafted through the house when Grandma made bread in the kitchen, and the sight of ducks waddling one by one to the pond, and the pleasure of playing hide-and-seek in the apple orchard—"Ah, if my children could only experience those memories." Then I have to remind myself that things weren't always so wonderful. The smell of baking bread had to compete with the pungent aroma of animal waste; there was a Cattle Crossing sign in front of my house that my friends used to tease me about; and, being in the country, we had no local convenience store we could run to whenever we needed a gallon of milk. Besides, those ducks could be a real pain when we had to chase them out of the barn. Face it, there are things about your past you could stand to do without. Likewise, there are things about your new lifestyle to celebrate.

"Being single isn't all bad!" Gary Richmond writes in his book, *Successful Single Parenting*.[2] Richmond, a clergyman from California, asked a group of single parents in one of his Sunday morning classes to describe the good side of singlehood. This is the list they came up with:

- I can squeeze the toothpaste in the middle, back, front—anywhere on the tube I want!
- I don't have to explain why I am late, and I am always late.
- I only have to make half of the bed.
- I no longer have to endure cold feet against my leg.
- I don't have to verify that the toilet seat is down before sitting.
- I can drink directly out of the milk carton.
- I don't have to go on a diet to support his efforts.
- I can run the air conditioner longer without being reminded what it costs.
- I can choose the TV station on Monday night.
- I don't have to pretend to like her parents anymore.
- I don't have to fold the towels in thirds anymore.
- I can belch after every meal!

An activity like this is one way that you might begin to use the anger you feel toward your situation to empower rather than drain yourself. In my own case, my initial feelings of helplessness at not being able to make ends meet made me angry, but I put my anger into positive overdrive when I started going to school. The nights when I was tired and didn't feel like attending class were the nights I had to use my anger to remind myself that I never wanted to be so helpless and vulnerable again. During my first few semesters, my energy came totally from anger. But instead of venting it toward my ex-husband or trying to get some sort of revenge—actions that in either case would have been unproductive—I simply used it to fuel my drive toward my goal of getting an education. Eventually, I reframed to the point where I was motivated by my personal satisfaction instead of anger, but it took time.

William Bridges, a consultant and authority on change, says the first step toward personal or business success is to acknowledge the losses and endings. He suggests we must first define what's over and what isn't. Just because you are now a single parent doesn't mean you have changed. Your marriage may be over, your loved one gone, your life turned upside down, but when it comes right down to it, you are still you. Bridges's advice is to "take a piece of the old way" with you. In other words, don't try to change everything in your life to forget the past; after all, it is your past that has made you who you are today. Evaluate your life and decide to keep some positive things intact (for example, favorite Saturday activities, favorite family dinners, favorite books, favorite music). This is also good advice to help your children adjust to the change. Let them keep a picture of their other parent in their rooms. Although you may want to forget the relationship, your children may want the comfort of knowing it was loving at one time.

Finally, there will not be a clear-cut time when you let go of the past and begin a new future. Sometimes you will feel in limbo, torn between the past and the future. Like those uncertain moments when a trapeze artist hangs suspended between one bar and another, it's a time when you will feel suspended between the security of the past and the uncertainty of the future. Bridges calls this time the "neutral zone." He says that most people don't understand the necessity of this time period and often expect to make a smooth transition from old to new. Even though this can be a difficult time, Bridges suggests it also be a time of creativity. "You need to capitalize on the opportunity that the neutral zone provides to do things differently and better."[3]

Create a list of traditions you and your family can use to define a new identity. Make these the trademarks of your single-parent family, something that will distinguish the old from the new. It will also help your kids in their transition to the new lifestyle by establishing new routines they can count on. Here is a list of possibilities:

- Take a trip to the library every Sunday afternoon.
- Dine out to celebrate payday. Choose a new restaurant each time.
- Have a family reading hour in your bed each night. (It beats watching TV!)
- Share funny stories each night at dinner time. Kids love to hear stories about when you were a child or when they were toddlers or babies. Show them you were a kid once, too.
- Schedule a movie and popcorn night, maybe the second Saturday of each month.

Step #1
Reframe the past.

- List positive aspects about your new single life.
- Continue some of the old ways; preserve the positive past.
- Create new traditions to mark the transition.

Letting Go of the Way Things "Should" Be

Our vision of what life "should" be like is formed from a variety of experiences, namely, what our parents taught us (by example or otherwise), interactions with religious groups, and various other influences from friends, relatives, television, newspapers, and so on. However, like Carol's story, life sometimes forces us to go against deeply ingrained values. This causes what psychologists call cognitive dissonance: a state of discomfort that occurs when there is a basic incompatibility between thoughts and actions, or between two or more sets of ideas, attitudes, or opinions that a person holds. In simpler terms, it's tough to believe one way and act another.

You may feel this kind of inconsistency between belief and behavior if you were taught that divorce is wrong, yet you left your abusive husband to start a new life. Maybe you've been taught that welfare recipients are lazy and irresponsible, yet you've had no other choice but to seek social services to survive. Quite possibly, you're someone like I was, who couldn't get beyond having anything less than a *Brady Bunch* or *Leave It to Beaver* existence. Whatever the dilemma, single parents are commonly faced with living a life that goes against the "shoulds."

I first learned how tough it was to accept the reality of my new life the time my ex came to pick the kids up for their first visitation after our divorce. Until just before that time, I had been a stay-at-home mom who occasionally worked part-time. During our marriage, their father wasn't home a lot because of the nature of his job. Consequently, I spent large blocks of time alone with my kids. I always knew where they were and what they were doing. I felt in control: I knew what they were watching on TV, who they were playing with in the neighborhood, what books they were reading and how many times a day they went to the bathroom.

Then everything fell apart. Before I knew it, my five- and seven-year-olds were walking out the front door to an unknown place with unknown neighbors and an unknown future. When my son turned around and asked, "Mommy, aren't you coming, too?" I held back the tears long enough to say, "No, honey, not this time." He walked away looking puzzled, knowing something was wrong with this picture, but not really knowing what. I spent the evening in tears, with an ache in my heart unmatched by anything I'd felt before. I wondered why I had to give up my children to the world at such a young age. I wasn't supposed to do this until they were at least seventeen or eighteen, right? This wasn't the way it was supposed to be.

Cindy had a similar experience when her son returned home one weekend with the news that his father's girlfriend had spent the night while he was there. Having been raised in a conservative Christian home, Cindy felt it was morally wrong for her ex-husband to have a sleeping partner while her son was in the house. This led to strong feelings of anger, guilt, and disappointment as she struggled to accept a situation over which she felt powerless.

When we're faced with this kind of dilemma, the type that leaves us feeling uncomfortable with a situation yet helpless to control it, the only answer is to find a way to make it fit within our own moral context. Relieving cognitive dissonance involves either changing the behavior or changing the belief. When changing the situation or behavior is not possible and changing the belief would be compromising an important part of your value system, reframing your attitude and accepting the situation is the only alternative.

To reframe my situation, I had to recognize the importance of the father-child relationship. As Shoshana Alexander put it in her book, *In Praise of Single Parents*, "There is always an Other."

Whether they are part of our daily lives or not, they are present in our children. The Other may be our children's biological parent or our adopted children's birth parents. The Other may be someone we once loved or someone we have never seen. Whether he or she is actively involved in the lives of our children or not, the Other is present in the nucleus of each cell of their bodies, present in the depths of their psyches. For our children, the Other is not "other" but part of them. And in whatever way and to whatever degree we can, we must honor their right to that part of themselves. For us that may well mean learning how to relate to and about that relationship with their other parent, whether that relationship is solely within our children's minds and imaginations or whether it also involves interaction between child and parent.[4]

Through reframing the situation, I was able to relinquish my expectations in order to provide a healthy reality for my kids. As much as I wanted to resist, I had to accept the fact that my kids had a right to know and love their father, and depriving them of that right would be taking away something very natural for them so I could resist what seemed unnatural for me.

In the same way, Cindy had to accept that she could not control her ex-husband's behavior, especially if he did not see it as morally wrong. The only thing she could do was commit to providing her son with the best example while he was in her home and hope he would someday choose her behavior over his father's. The opportunity for Cindy's son to see two different lifestyles and make his own decision about which was right or wrong was not all bad. Painful? Yes. Hopeless? No.

Because of the way we've been raised or values we choose to adhere to, we too often beat ourselves up for not living up to our own or others' expectations. It's important to recognize that it is sometimes necessary to overlook expectations in order to deal with the realities life throws at us. By this recognition, we can avoid the consequences of expecting too much from life.

Dr. Richard Gotti, a practicing psychotherapist and coauthor of *Overcoming Regret*, says an obstacle that keeps us from moving on with our lives after a disappointing event is "contained in what may be the mind's most outrageous assumption—that it is really possible to be perfect." Once you are able to accept that "we are all blunderers," as novelist Edith Wharton once put it, you will find comfort in learning from your mistakes and feel less compelled to live up to anyone's standards besides your own. Gotti says striving for an image of perfection breeds disappointment and self-blaming regret. "Trying to live up to an unattainable image cuts us off from our true needs and feelings. The danger to our well-being is that the fantasy person can become more real to us than who we really are."[5]

The last thing you need is an unrealistic view of yourself or the world around you. Dwelling on the way things should be is a clear indication that you are still trying to fulfill an unrealistic fantasy or you are trying to live according to someone else's expectations. Wanting the storybook life is natural, but no one ever truly experiences it. Such is the perfect little family of four who walks into the church on Sunday morning with pretty clothing and clean, smiling faces. A single mother sitting in the pew next to them glances over in envy. "Oh, to have what they have. They seem so happy and full of joy." Little does she know of the struggles that went on at their home that morning. "I don't want to go to church," yelled the son. "I don't know what to wear," sighed the wife. "He's hitting me," screamed the daughter. "Everybody just shut up," said the husband, as they all drove into the church parking lot. We've all heard about it and many of us have lived it. I haven't met a perfect family yet, and now that I've experienced a quite imperfect one, I'm no longer under the delusion that perfection exists. But I am convinced that taking off the rose-colored glasses and facing reality is what really allows us to grow and mature. My new marriage and family life is full of real situations. I'm happy, not because we're perfect, but simply because we're real. That is all I've come to expect from myself and those around me.

Step #2
Reframe your expectations.

- Identify the inconsistencies.
- Find a way to make it right.
- Take pleasure in your "real" existence.

Discovering Joy in the Way Things Are

Poet and essayist Devorah Major writes eloquently about her single-parent family in her essay "A Cord Between Us."

> Through my first years as a single parent, following the terror of an ugly and sometimes violent breakup and the painful death of what once had promised to be a wonderful life-long friendship, my children and I built a stronger and deeper kinship. It seemed as though in the painful lesson of learning that all promises could be broken and nothing could

be taken for granted—not even the resiliency of love—we had learned how to be better friends to one another. . . .

Somewhere in between the hard questions which they asked for years and the hard answers which I sought to give them, sometime in those months when I could not hide my fragility, my weaknesses, my pain, my imperfections, I had grown, we had grown into a stronger unit. I was, after all, the parent who stayed. I was the one who had not missed a birthday, who tried and usually succeeded in fulfilling, although often late, every promise I made, and I was the one who had learned, feet to the coals, how to be humble in the face of my children's clear-eyed perceptions. And I had, thankfully, remembered to remind them again and again that no matter what else, these two were always wanted, always loved, always desired by their parents. And so my daughter, my son and I lay cuddling the morning, finishing each other's sentences, jumping into corners of conversation, having all the time in the world to be friends. . . .

So when weeks later I lay in my bed on an ordinary, special morning feeling my daughter slowly cool, teaching my son to be quiet, laughing, I took the time to enjoy the rewards of my single life. . . . Friendship is not a reward for the courage or foolishness or even the necessity of single parenting. But there is a special friendship that grows, like adult friendships grow, from simply being together more of the time, from finding the answers, looking at the questions and leaning one on the other. We are closer and together our hearts have grown.[6]

I was close to tears when I first read this excerpt because I, like Major, had come to a realization after many agonizing, tearful nights that my relationship with my children had a special ingredient I never felt with my parents or I never witnessed in my married friends' families. Not that it made single parenthood some sort of panacea, but it added a richness to my life that made me proud of my role.

Statistically, single parents have a tougher time meeting financial, emotional, and physical needs than two-parent or childless families. Indeed, 60 percent of all single mothers earn less than $20,000 annually. Few of them have court-ordered child support agreements. Many of them work more than one job, earning only the minimum wage at each. Not only does the financial stress cause emotional and sometimes physical pain, but added complications like shared custody arrangements, disagreeable relationships with ex-spouses, and numerous other details magnify the feelings of helplessness. Taking all of this into consideration, it is not difficult to see why a single mother would feel less than excited about her future prospects and resent her negative lifestyle.

A friend of mine called me complaining about how she just couldn't get ahead. It seemed that every time she started to crawl out of the hole, something else came around to knock her back in. Interestingly enough, though, she followed her complaints with, "I guess I should be thankful. My kids are more responsible now than they've ever been . . . and they seem to really understand how hard it is for me. We've all become more honest with each other. Money can't buy that." Although she needed to unload some of her frustration, she clearly understood the positive impact her parenting was having on her relationship with her kids.

I honestly believe that realizing I alone was responsible for parenting and fearing I might not do everything right made me a better parent. I began to look at everything in my life in the context of how it would affect my children. In doing that, I was constantly aware of my actions and the messages I was sending my kids daily. In being forced to examine my behavior, I ultimately changed it. I became more relaxed. I began having fun at home, not worrying about whether I was doing everything perfectly or not. I found I was able to enjoy parenting as a labor of love instead of a burden. Parenting on my own made me feel proud. I slowly began to hold my head high and pronounce, "Yes, I'm a single parent and I love it!"

If you are able to turn your thinking around and feel genuine pride in your family and its strengths, you are well on your way to taking positive action.

Step #3
Reframe the present.

- Cherish friendship with your kids.
- Recognize the positive impact on them.
- Turn the pain into pride.

In a Nutshell

"A picture is worth a thousand words," someone once said, but you can be sure that no two people will perceive the same thousand words when they look at a picture. How you perceive a picture is much the same as how you perceive life in general. You will judge it based on your experiences, your upbringing, and your knowledge of the world. Similarly, your single-parent family portrait may look a bit empty or tarnished, but upon closer examination, a simple richness might be discovered. Unfortunately, our limited perceptions can often keep us from experiencing the richest rewards.

Egon Friedell said, "Clothe an idea in words and it loses its freedom of movement." Some things are better left unexplained, subject to personal interpretation. You may feel frustrated because of the lack of a clear-cut explanation for each facet of your new lifestyle, but if you keep an open mind, you just might discover "freedom of movement." With this newfound freedom, the sky is the limit. By the end of chapter 3, you may even be inclined to proudly hang your newly framed portrait for the world to see. You can start by opening your eyes to all the possibilities.

Checkpoint

- Have you listed positive aspects about your new single life?
- Have you created new traditions to mark the transition?
- Have you identified the inconsistencies between your beliefs and your behavior?
- Have you taken action to reconcile the inconsistencies?
- Are you taking pleasure in your real existence?
- Are you identifying a new bond, or friendship, with your kids?
- Have you listed the positive impacts your new life will have on your children?
- Are you beginning to turn pain into pride?

If you can answer yes to all these questions, go on to chapter 3.

3

TURNING NEGATIVE ENERGY INTO POSITIVE STEPS

We could never learn to be brave and patient if there were only joy in the world. —Helen Keller

Finding the Silver Lining

Gary and his ten-year-old son, Chris, romp around their West Virginia home doing things fathers and sons do together—playing games, tinkering with the car, talking about sports. At first glance, their light-hearted interaction and tough-guy antics seem evidence of a normal family life. But when Gary begins to talk about the last eight years, it is clear a background of pain and heartache undergirds their present existence.

"Paula and I had Chris when we were teenagers," Gary remembers. "By the time Chris was two and a half, our poverty and lack of experience had stressed the marriage. She became very disinterested in raising Chris, and spent more and more time away from home with friends—partying, doing drugs, and sleeping.

"When the end came, there was no custody battle. I was naturally the care-taker over the second and third years of his life. This left me with most of the chores, all the bills, and a child to potty train." Gary initially worried he would not be able to support himself, and he feared facing life alone.

"I went to college full-time after the divorce, borrowing all the money I could, and spent five years getting my degree in science," Gary explains. "It was tough, but I didn't ever want to feel that sense of helplessness again, especially where Chris's welfare was concerned. Getting the degree didn't mean financial independence for us by any stretch of the imagination, but it did give me the confidence to know I had choices in the job market. Taking Chris to daycare every day was a tough decision during that time because he was so young. However, I felt I had little choice; it was poverty or school.

"Now, I'm less concerned about money, even though my debt has increased ten-fold. I spend every penny to survive, save what I can, and pray someday the debt I have won't crush me. But we are here. I have a decent place to live, a working car; we eat what we want and stay warm."

Gary said being a very young single parent made it tough to find understanding peers. "You are not alone when you have a child, physically, but I had no friends. There was an aloneness in my mind and heart that a child could not fill. I was unable to date like most young men. My friends were childless at the time and couldn't relate. In these last few years, though, I don't fear loneliness anymore. I am content being without a partner, content being a dad. I like raising my plants, cat, child, and coaching basketball."

Gary admits life was not easy for the first several years. He always had a dream of going to medical school, so he took a chance and left his son, then six, with his ex-wife one summer so he could pursue his dream. He was horrified when Chris returned from his summer stay with stories of sexual abuse involving neighbors and older children. Gary decided then to put his dream on hold until he could approach it with peace of mind.

"I tried going the third semester, but I was unable to put the time in and had many problems of my own. I left school to work and care for Chris. We spent months in counseling trying to return to some kind of normalcy. Chris became suicidal, highly reactive and defensive—he had lost his spirit."

"One time in a rage of anger, resentment, and sadness, Chris destroyed his fish tank with a large block of wood. In the process, the fish went sprawling all over the floor along with twenty gallons of water. Rather than react in a frantic, angered parent mode, I paused. He was throwing the fit for something small, yet I knew his emotions were about so many other things."

Gary knew he had to control himself if he was going to teach Chris anything. "I remember calmly mopping the floor as he watched, expressing my disappointment. My choice at the time was not to go to a great effort to save the fish—that was a consequence he had to deal with as a result of the broken tank. I was mopping the floor to prevent the landlord from causing me future problems—and I made this clear to Chris. He later helped clean up the glass and other stuff, mentioning how sorry he was for killing the fish. In that moment he saw the absurdity and lack of control of his emotions. Years later, he now has a tank that he takes care of with minimal supervision. Dead fish taught him a lesson about controlling emotions and learning responsibility. Who would have thought?"

Negative emotions played an important part in their family life, but Gary said it enabled them to grow together.

"My depression and resentment toward Paula were often felt by Chris, no matter how well I hid those feelings," recounts Gary. "He would sometimes feel guilty about the divorce, thinking it was his fault. I have spent many hours building his self-esteem and talking with him about how and why things are the way they are. I have shared with him how his parents are growing up, too, in a very complicated and changing world—how we are all learning to be better people.

"In retrospect, I had two choices concerning what to do with all that negative energy: I could either continue to use these emotions, to take from other people, or I could find ways to create experiences that would generate positive emotions. Obviously, I chose to create rather than to take, but it took me a while to recognize I even had a choice. Once you can get to that recognition point, it all becomes so much richer and easier."

For example, Gary said he used his ex-wife's drug problem as a teaching experience for his son. "I could have pretended my ex-wife did not have a problem, never talking about it and hating her for it. But then I would have not allowed the negative experience to have positive value. Although Chris suffers when faced with the truth about his mother, he now is aware of the destructiveness drugs cause—something many young adults have not grasped. This awareness all came from having frank, truthful conversations with my child and allowing negative situations to present themselves, within safe limits, for a learning experience."

Gary says approaching life this way can be a frightening experience, and takes a certain amount of faith in following parental instincts. "A very wise friend of mine says it this way: 'In parenting, there is always an opportunity at some later time to make use of uncomfortable, negative, and maybe even horrible experiences to promote growth, happiness, and responsibility. The key is in learning to see the moments when they arise and having the faith that transformation can occur.'"

❀❀❀❀❀❀❀❀❀❀

Chapter 1 helped you conquer fear; chapter 2 taught you how to reframe your situation. This chapter is about action. Once you decide that you're not going to let fear rule your life and you really can survive in your new role, it's time to turn your newly found confidence into positive action. It's time to become a sponge, so to speak, soaking up all the knowledge you can and using it to make things happen. This will be the stage when you will expend a lot of energy without seeing immediate results. It's a stage when most people will begin to second-guess themselves. Some may even quit trying. Expect this to be your most challenging time, but also expect to find it the most rewarding.

According to one of Newton's laws of physics, for every action, there is an equal and opposite reaction. You've also heard there is an evil force to counteract every good deed. What you might not have been told until you became a single parent, however, is that it takes about a thousand watts of positive energy to counteract a few negative charges. It seems especially difficult to counteract the anger we feel after losing a spouse or the disappointment we experience when we realize how challenging the single-parenting lifestyle can be. As a result, we have a natural tendency to allow the anger or disappointment to control our lives, because it is simply easier to succumb to the feelings than to do something about them. Parenting alone is not an easy task, especially when it's overshadowed by negative energy like anger, guilt, disappointment, depression, or pain. It is important that you allow yourself time to heal before expecting these feelings to subside. In the meantime, however, don't let them paralyze you. It's easy to let negative feelings become the excuse for not taking positive steps toward success.

While you must maintain a healthy respect for the necessity of these emotions in your life for a period of time, you must also appreciate their usefulness toward fueling a positive journey.

In one of my favorite novels, *Hinds' Feet on High Places,* author Hannah Hurnard relates an allegorical tale about the ugly and deformed Much-Afraid and her journey to high places with the Great Shepherd. Much-Afraid, in her attempt to escape her treacherous family, the Fearings, agrees to travel with the Shepherd to the top of a mountain (the High Places), where he promises she will be transformed both physically and spiritually. Wanting her new being, yet not understanding what she must go through to get there, she fearfully accepts the challenge and agrees to trust fully in his guidance. One of the first things the Shepherd does is assigns Sorrow and Suffering to be Much-Afraid's companions on her upward journey. Her response is typical of what many of us have exclaimed during our times of pain.

> "I can't go with them," she gasped. "I can't! I can't! O my Lord Shepherd, why do you do this to me? How can I travel in their company? It is more than I can bear. You tell me that the mountain way itself is so steep and difficult that I cannot climb it alone. Then why, oh why, must you make Sorrow and Suffering my companions? Couldn't you have given Joy and Peace to go with me, to strengthen me and encourage me and help me on the difficult way? I never thought you would do this to me!" And she burst into tears.

Much-Afraid discovered through her journey that Sorrow and Suffering were her greatest sources of strength. They quietly walked with her, sometimes with an unbearable eeriness, and guided her through the rough terrain. Often one went before her, while the other followed, to keep Much-Afraid from running ahead or turning back. Toward the end of her journey, shortly before she reached the top of the mountain, Much-Afraid changed her mind about her companions.

> In some strange way she began to feel that they were becoming real friends, and not just attendants whom the Shepherd had commanded to go with her as guides and helpers. She found, too, that now she was accepting their companionship and in this way she seemed more alive than ever before to beauty and delight in the world around her. It seemed as though her senses had been quickened in some extraordinary

way, enabling her to enjoy every little detail of her life; so that although her companions actually were Sorrow and Suffering, she often felt an almost inexplicable joy and pleasure at the same time.[1]

As Gary related in his story, there's nothing more satisfying and rewarding than to use these seemingly negative emotions as teachers and friends in making progress. It involves moving to a new level of self-awareness—something few human beings attain without significant strain and struggle. If you think the road to a successful and healthy existence seems too long and bumpy for the reward, think again; the road you're traveling now is probably going in circles. Although it may feel familiar with no surprises, the scenery will eventually begin to frustrate and bore you, and life will, as they say, pass you by. Fear and an old way of thinking are the two main obstacles keeping you from taking a new road. I've shown you how to face them both. Now it's time to harness all your energy, from both positive and negative sources, and move on.

Remember the long-term goals we talked about in chapter 1? We're now going to begin planning and enacting the specific steps toward reaching those goals. Although it sounds intimidating, this conscious attempt to plan the details of your excursion will test your commitment to each goal and will give you a chance to change your mind before you invest further time or energy in them.

I Don't Think I Have What It Takes!

Christine and her eight-year-old daughter, Jenna, moved to a small one-bedroom apartment after Christine and Jenna's father divorced. Christine's waitressing job in a resort town was sporadic. During slow times, she barely made enough money to make ends meet. During peak seasons, however, she made significantly more. Christine desperately wanted to buy a home with a yard so Jenna could have a puppy and a larger play area. She also wanted Jenna to have the luxury of sleeping in her own room. Above all, Christine wanted to begin building equity in her own home, rather than throwing her money away on rent. She wanted to feel in control of her future—something she hadn't felt for a long time.

She became depressed when a loan officer told her she didn't make enough steady income to afford a home. She had no other job skills, and her hours at the restaurant enabled her to work while Jenna was in school or when Jenna's grandparents were available to watch her. Christine couldn't see a way out. Getting another job meant going to a schedule that might require paying for Jenna's daycare; staying where she was meant not ever owning the home she wanted. Christine's bitterness toward her ex-husband intensified. She began to rationalize her negative situation by blaming him. She also blamed herself for trying to make it work with him for so many years. "If I had gotten out sooner, when Jenna was a baby, I could have gone to school or done something to improve myself," she thought, feeling angry and guilty for not being able to provide her daughter with a more secure lifestyle.

Although enthralled in pain and resentment, Christine possessed all she needed for the journey toward success:

1. an intense love for her daughter
2. a vision of a realistic destination
3. a reason and the determination to succeed

Christine's desire to own a home was driven by the love she had for her daughter, as well as a need to prove her independence. She often said, "If it were only me, this old apartment would be just fine. But I want more for Jenna." This is a completely natural, healthy feeling that many parents experience. We always want our children to feel safe and secure in our care. Even when they may already feel safe and secure because of the love we show, we still long to provide a certain environment, to make ourselves feel better about the job we're doing.

There's nothing wrong with wanting more for our children. Wanting to provide the best possible circumstances for our family is a healthy goal, worthy of our efforts. We all know that we'll never regret loving our children too much (not to be confused with giving too much) or working hard to provide for them (not to be confused with always working). Therefore, Christine's love for Jenna is a motivation powerful enough to help her maintain her focus on the journey.

Step #1
Substitute exterior negatives with inner positives.

- Recognize your natural parenting instincts as strengths.
- Base your ability to succeed on your motivation of love, not anger.
- Focus on the future with that love and motivation in mind.

Devising a Plan

As we mentioned in chapter 1, it's tough to start on a journey without a plan. When was the last time you got into your car without having a clue as to where you were going? Okay, I know sometimes driving around with no destination in mind is a good way to burn off anger or frustration, but under normal circumstances, getting in the car is a clear sign you have somewhere to go. Likewise, don't start your expedition without a clear picture of your destination. Don't conjure up an unrealistic picture of your journey's end, either. You can get in your car and decide you're going to the French Riviera, but I guarantee you won't get there without a significant amount of money and a boat or plane to boot. Therefore, before you embark on your journey,

- choose your destination, and
- map out specific stopping, or reevaluation, points along the way.

For whatever reason, Christine has a picture in her mind of what she wants for her single-parent family. Quite possibly, Christine grew up in a modest, small-town atmosphere, and her memories of a secure family situation cause her to want the same for her child. Or, on the contrary, maybe Christine was raised in a big-city tenement, and her memories are shadowed by insecurities or fear. If so, her desire to provide something different for her child has created the picture in her mind.

Whatever your goals or desires for your family, your mental picture of your journey's end is a direct result of your past experiences and your perception of happiness. This picture will be different for everyone. The important thing is that your picture be congruent with your values and life principles. Don't let go of it. As you go along in your journey, you'll most likely refine it. In fact, when you get close to achieving it, it may be completely different from the original picture you had in mind. Nevertheless, you must start with something. Even if it seems like a fairy tale to you now, hold on to it. Write down the details of your picture. For example, Christine would write,

I want a nice three-bedroom home in an area where it will be safe for Jenna to play outside. Soon after moving in, we'll get a puppy. Jenna will meet new friends in her neighborhood and go to a good school. We'll be able to sit out on our front porch at night and listen to the radio or watch the cars and neighbors go by. We won't have to worry about hearing the couple upstairs fighting or the lady next door snoring. I'll be proud to invite my friends over to our new home, and I'll feel strong and independent when a date comes to pick me up for dinner or a movie. Jenna will have her own bedroom to fix up in little-girl style, and I'll finally enjoy the privacy of a good cry in my own space. We'll be happy, and Jenna will have good memories of life with mom!

Note that Christine does not write that she wants a 5,000-square-foot mansion in Beverly Hills. She understands that material possessions will not bring her happiness; rather, it is the symbolism and meaning of attaining her goal that will bring her the most peace of mind. She writes down all the reasons a home of her own would make her feel good, from a parenting as well as a personal perspective.

Note also that, although the underlying anger she feels toward her ex-husband may motivate her to prove that she does not need him, she focuses her writing on the positive and productive reasons for wanting a home of her own. If she could, Christine would need to reexamine whether or not the goal is a worthy one.

Christine may play this picture over and over in her mind, and even feel at times that it is nothing more than an unattainable dream. There are no guarantees that she'll get what she wants. There is one guarantee, however: if she doesn't take any action to get there, it will always be a figment of her imagination.

Step #2
Picture positive results.

- Know where you're going before you begin.
- Balance your dreams with realistic expectations.
- Be sure you're motivated by inner peace, not revenge.

Harnessing the Energy So It Won't Explode

Christine's determination to put her plan into action is noble, but not yet absent of negative energy. This isn't all bad, since the journey merely requires energy, in any form. A complete lack of energy signals depression, which would be a much deeper problem. Any energy, positive or negative, is power. However, unchecked negative energy can be self-destructive if not dealt with honestly and firmly.

When people experience anger or bitterness, they generally need to do something with it. Some people try to get revenge by venting their negative feelings toward the person they feel is responsible for their misfortune. Others keep their feelings bottled up, hoping they'll go away if they just forget about them. But neither of these responses will bring positive results. Those who seek revenge almost always end up hurting others. And as much as we think vengeance will bring us satisfaction, it almost always causes us more pain and suffering. Likewise, keeping feelings bottled up is simply a form of procrastination that also inevitably increases pain and suffering. Someday, somewhere, those feelings will come out. It may happen years down the road with another spouse or partner, or it may come out as anger toward our children when they blossom into teenagers. Bottling anger only makes us time bombs set to go off at the next turn of uncomfortable events. Obviously, the best way to deal with negative emotions is to confront them head-on and use them to create positive results.

At first it may seem unhealthy to use negative feelings to fuel a new endeavor, and it could very well become unhealthy if those feelings never become neutralized by positive results. But chances are, once positive things start happening as a result of your life-changing decisions, the negative feelings will begin to subside. As Much-Afraid discovered by walking daily with Sorrow and

Suffering, you, too, will find pleasure in using your darker emotions to effect bright changes. You'll begin to pity the people you once held in contempt. You may even begin to understand their helplessness and see why they might have wronged you or treated you unfairly. As you discover and accept yourself, you'll acquire the gift of accepting others for who they are. You'll become more and more confident of your ability to achieve success and less and less likely to blame others for your failures. As Stephanie Dowrick writes in *Intimacy and Solitude*, "People who have been pushed by circumstance or constitution to question who they are and what their place is in the world, often under really tough conditions, frequently have a richness of vision less apparent in those whose lives have been freer of inner conflict."[2] If you approach your journey knowing it will have its ups and downs, and if you give yourself the time you need to complete it, the transformation of negative energy into positive will be subtle, yet highly noticeable to those around you.

I remember my friends telling me what a change they had seen in my attitude over a period of several months. I began attending night classes at the local community college because I was determined to make a better life for myself and my family. I initially doubted my ability to actually get a degree, but I was so disgusted with my inability to pay the bills and my inadequate employment that I just started doing something to make myself feel like I was going to change it all. I admit I went through the blaming process like everyone else: if only my ex-husband would have done this or that; if only my employer would be more sympathetic; if only, if only, if only.

Not surprisingly, as I drew closer to my goal, I was captured by a love for learning and found myself working for the degree because I wanted the personal fulfillment. In the end, the life I was able to create for myself became the icing on the cake. The goal never changed, but my reason for wanting it was totally transformed. When all was said and done, I could attribute my success to the systematic approach I followed to conquer my fears, reframe the picture, and embark on a journey with a realistic end.

Step #3
Neutralize the negative with positive action.

- Face your negative emotions, and appreciate their existence.
- Allow them to teach and guide you through change.
- Quit blaming and start doing!

Getting Started

"Where do I begin?" is the question most asked by single parents when confronted with making decisions about the future. Determining priorities and seeking professional advice are the basic starting points. As we discussed in Chapter 1, short-term goals can be accomplished by prioritizing them and getting someone else involved who can be objective about your situation. This holds true when you are embarking on the journey toward long-term fulfillment as well. Since you are devising a plan that includes periodic stopping or reevaluation points, it only makes sense to treat each of those points as a short-term goal leading to the ultimate long-term plan. Therefore, take each point one at a time and arm yourself with the tools, people, and appropriate mindset to get yourself to the first checkpoint.

Let's explore this concept with a brief analysis of Christine's situation and her course of action.

The Facts

1. Christine's income is low and erratic, affecting her ability to buy a home.
2. Flexible hours on her current job allow her to avoid paid daycare.
3. Christine has no formal education, limiting her employment possibilities.
4. Going to school part-time takes money from the budget and time away from Jenna.
5. Christine's credit history is less than ideal, also hindering her ability to buy a home.

The Priorities

Before doing anything, Christine must decide what is most important to her and what is best for Jenna. This is when moral choices and the question of priorities are most critical, priorities like the following:

1. Is Christine motivated by appearances, or a true longing for inner peace?
2. What is Christine willing to sacrifice, and for how long, to attain her goal?
3. Will the sacrifices of time and money to get an education jeopardize Christine's relationship with Jenna?

In my experience, goals motivated by image rather than self-fulfillment do not withstand the rigorous demands of persistence and perseverance. To put it another way, you'll quit before you get there if you're motivated by the wrong reasons. In this particular case, Christine must weigh her need to provide a loving and encouraging family atmosphere for her daughter against her longing for self-acceptance and approval from her peers. If there is a comfortable balance, Christine can probably count on having enough energy to complete her mission.

Another factor to consider is that her education will take a great sacrifice of time and money. Christine must balance the effects that her strained resources will have on both herself and her daughter against the possibility of getting a higher-paying job. Christine may decide that going back to school is not the answer and that other job possibilities that can help her achieve her desired goal are within grasp. Once she has determined what she is willing to sacrifice and for how long, Christine is mentally and morally equipped to chart her course of action.

The Decisions

With regard to her education, Christine concludes she has three choices.

1. Going to school full-time during the day, while working part-time. This will delay her buying a home until after she finishes her schooling, which could take two to five years, depending on what career she decides to pursue. By that time, Jenna will be entering her teen years.
2. Continue working full-time while going to school part-time. She might need seven to ten years to finish school, which is unacceptable because she feels she will sacrifice a lot of time with her daughter and may still be unable to purchase a home until Jenna is almost eighteen, defeating the

purpose of her original goal.

3. Find a job now that offers higher income opportunities and more security, so she can purchase a home in a shorter period of time.

Although Christine would still like to pursue a meaningful career by getting a higher education, it will not help her achieve the short term goal of buying a home. In light of this, she is willing to look at the current job market first to see if there are any agreeable possibilities that might enhance her future career and offer her the immediate cash she needs to become a homeowner.

In changing her way of thinking, Christine discovers a hidden blessing, yet another benefit of turning negative energy into positive steps. She knows that if she finds a job where she can work weekdays, she will be able to spend the entire weekend with Jenna. Plus, she will only have to rely on paid daycare for the two to three hours Jenna will be free after school. Christine's parents have been watching Jenna on the weekends while Christine works at the restaurant, but they both work during the week and wouldn't be able to help with Jenna after school. Christine decides to check into other alternatives for after-school daycare.

Christine also decides to begin working on straightening out some of the black marks on her credit history. The divorce wreaked havoc on her finances for a while and miscommunication during the separation period resulted in some debts going unpaid. Since then, Christine has not had much luck with getting credit, but is paying off the creditors she currently has in a timely manner. She recognizes that addressing this problem will improve how she feels about herself, as well as be a positive step toward obtaining a mortgage loan someday.

The Positive Perspective

Now that Christine has made decisions based on what she feels is best for her and her daughter, she must decide to harness her negative feelings toward her life, her ex-husband, and the mortgage company, and use them as her motivation for accomplishing something and not as an excuse for staying where she is. She has taken the first step in creating a positive situation instead of taking from others to provide her alibi. Next, she needs to see the long-term goal as the eradicator of the things she feels are currently controlling her. Once she gets a house, she will no longer have to deal with the mortgage company's rejection. Once she finds a better job and is feeling more confident, she will no longer hear the ringing of her ex-husband's put-downs in her mind. Once she has set a goal and achieved something positive, she will no longer view her lifestyle as merely surviving.

Some call it an "I'll show them" attitude, but I prefer to call it an attitude of higher thinking—an attitude that rises above the average thought processes, one that values choices, knowledge and self-discovery. Every time I hear a single mom blame her ex-husband for her current problems, I find myself thinking (and sometimes saying), "As long as you continue to blame him, he is still in control of your life." I know it's tough in the beginning, but quit blaming and start finding your own way. It'll be exhilarating, I promise.

Christine's Course of Action

I. Determine priorities:
    Owning a home
    Spending time with Jenna
    Job fulfillment
    Quality daycare
II. Make decisions:
    Look for weekday employment
    Look at educational options
    Check into alternative daycare
    Find a good balance
III. Get the proper perspective:
    Maintain original focus
    Use the negative as the reason, no the excuse
    Eradicate the negative

In a Nutshell

Dr. Viktor Frankl spent many years as a prisoner at Auschwitz and other concentration camps during World War II. His ability to separate himself from his surroundings during this time was phenomenal. He believed that "everything can be taken from a man but one thing: to choose one's attitude in any given set of circumstances." Human suffering, according to Frankl is relative, as he wrote in his book, *Man's Search for Meaning.*

> A man's suffering is similar to the behavior of gas. If a certain quantity of gas is pumped into an empty chamber, it will fill the chamber completely and evenly, no matter how big the chamber. Thus suffering completely fills the human soul and conscious mind, no matter whether the suffering is great or little. Therefore the "size" of human suffering is absolutely relative.[3]

While the suffering of a prisoner in a Nazi concentration camps is unquestionably greater than the suffering of a single parent who cannot provide adequately for his or her child, the feelings of helplessness, depression, anger, and sorrow engulf a person's heart with a similar vigor and totality. The choice to be victimized or to wage a personal victory is largely up to the individual. Turning negative energy into positive action takes conscious decision-making, but more importantly it requires a shift from placing blame to taking responsibility. Make like the famous commercial, and just do it.

Checkpoint

- Have you substituted exterior negatives with interior positives (parental love, vision, reason)?
- Have you identified your parenting instincts as strengths?
- Can you focus on the future with love as your driving force?
- Have you written down your vision for the future?
    Does it include realistic expectations?
    Is it based on inner peace congruent with your value system?
- Have you identified your negative emotions?
    Do you appreciate their value in your healing process?
    Have you thought of ways they can help you through change?
- Are you ready to stop blaming and start doing?

    If you can answer yes to all these questions, go on to chapter 4.

PART TWO:

Self-Development

4

LEARNING NEW SKILLS

We must overcome the notion that we must be regular. It robs us of the chance to be extraordinary and leads us to the mediocre.

—Uta Hagen

Overcoming Obstacles

At thirty years old, Danita beams with pride when she talks about all the obstacles she's overcome in the last few years. At one time, everything seemed to be going against her. Unlike her single-mother counterparts, Danita did not let the usual stereotypical adjectives (black, woman, undereducated, welfare mother) keep her at the bottom. An attractive and energetic young mother, she relates her story with a genuine hope of helping other single mothers overcome racial, gender, and economic barriers.

Danita's story began at age fifteen, when she met the "man of her dreams." Like so many others, the young relationship led to an unexpected pregnancy and the birth of a child, Yvonne, when Danita was only seventeen. Under pressure from her family, Danita married her child's father. However, the teen marriage began deteriorating when reality set in.

According to Danita, youth and inexperience created a communication barrier, which kept them from sharing their lives with one another. Their second child, Brittany, came five years later. When Danita's husband started disappearing periodically and was showing signs of drug abuse, she tried to save her marriage by being more attentive.

"I was fighting so hard to make it work, she said, because I didn't think I could go it alone. At least that's what my mom and my grandma had me believing. They would quote the Bible to me, telling me I should try to work things out in my marriage. But deep down I knew God hadn't intended for me to suffer like I was."

A year after Brittany's birth, the couple had their third child, Bianca. It soon became clear to Danita that her attentiveness could not save her marriage. Their problems were more deeply rooted. By now, her husband had quit his job and was heavy into the drug scene. She had no choice but to move her family into public housing and go on welfare.

"Eventually, I listened to my heart and filed for a divorce. My husband fought me for two years and refused to sign the papers. Since I couldn't afford an attorney, I had to wait until he was ready. The day he signed, I felt like a new woman. I discovered all I really needed was to get rid of the negative force in my life. From then on, I started rediscovering the confident, strong-willed child I once was. Fortunately, the strong will and determination my grandparents had taught me while I was growing up would be what kept me going as a single parent."

In an effort to change her life, Danita discovered a reentry program at her local community college designed to help single parents and displaced homemakers learn new skills and find productive jobs. Her contagious enthusiasm for learning eventually led to a paid position at the reentry center. Danita recounts her days on the job:

"I remember getting upset with one of my coworkers because she was in a bad mood and taking it out on some of the applicants. She commented about 'those welfare mothers,' and I about went through the roof. I reminded her that I was one of 'those mothers' and if it hadn't been for the help of someone at the center, I wouldn't have had the confidence to try. The women coming into the center were down as low as they could be. I knew they were taking their very first step toward helping themselves. It was important to greet them with a positive attitude. I was afraid if I didn't, they might leave and never come back."

One day Danita's boss asked her to help promote a new program introducing women to nontraditional jobs in the workplace. They wanted to spark new interest in male-dominated fields through learning seminars and hands-on experience. Danita agreed and soon became interested in one of the professions.

"Every Saturday, we would take a group of women to one of the local union offices," she explained. "One week we visited the pipefitters union; the next week, maybe the heavy equipment operators union. There would always be a speaker and a demonstration session for all the women to observe and try a specialized skill. I'll never forget the day we went to the sheet metal workers union. There was this flat piece of sheet metal laying on the table, and the instructor held up a tool box and said, 'This is what we're gonna make today.' I looked at him and said, 'Yeah, right.' Because of that comment, he stayed with me, probably to prove me wrong. I made that tool box and I still have it at home to remind me that something useful can be made from what looks like a useless piece of sheet metal."

The instructor, who has since passed away, recognized a special quality in Danita that caused him to want to work with her further. "It was his confidence that kept me going through the whole process," she said. "I wish he was around today to see how far I've come."

Danita said she got so excited after making the tool box that she knew this was the trade for her. She discovered that one of the reasons women weren't attracted to the sheet metal trade was because they were intimidated by the math portion of the applicants' test. "When I found that out, I just laughed and said, 'Is that all?' The money and the benefits also attracted me. I knew this was more than just a chance to get off the welfare system and make it on my own; it was a chance to do something creative and enjoyable."

Danita pursued the trade and succeeded in landing an apprentice position early in her training. She said there were some obstacles she had to overcome as a black woman, but when everyone "removed their walls," she discovered some valuable friendships.

"I was probably my biggest enemy because I went into it expecting to be treated like an incompetent woman. Everyone on the job was male and my boss was a thirty-five-year-old white man. Right away, I made assumptions about him and my coworkers. I developed a superwoman attitude and was determined to prove I didn't need them. The problem was, as an apprentice, I very much needed their help. As a result, their reaction to my attitude was stereotypical. We had a rough couple of months."

"As I began to show my willingness to work hard, and they began showing their willingness to teach me what I needed to know, we became good friends, like a family. One day my car broke down and I was frantic not knowing how to reach anyone on the job to let them know I would be late. When I got there, they didn't chew me out. They were genuinely worried about me, and several people gave me their phone numbers in case I ever had trouble like that again. I felt great. I had gained their respect and made some good friends."

Danita, who is now practicing her trade atop one of the tallest hotel/casino resorts in the world, agrees that her story is out of the ordinary. But she strongly believes that many women can overcome stereotypical attitudes if they are willing to put forth the effort. "If we're going to change perceptions, we have to be willing to take out-of-the-ordinary action. That's why I continue to tell my story through volunteer work at the reentry center. I know other mothers will hear it and say, 'Hey, if she can do it, so can I'—that's what it's all about."

❈❈❈❈❈❈❈❈❈❈

According to the most recent government statistics, 44 percent of all single mothers in 1991 had no child support award from the courts. Nearly half, or about 4.5 million, of these families lived in poverty. Of those who did have court-ordered child support agreements, 12 percent didn't receive one dime. The statistics also report custodial mothers were about two and a half times as likely to be in poverty as custodial fathers, and more than four times as likely as married couples.

In addition, government programs have traditionally encouraged single parents to stay in poverty rather than work their way out. In the past, the welfare system has rewarded parents for having more children (the more children, the more benefits), not for increasing their marketability in the workplace. But as we go to press, federal and state agencies are in the process of reforming their welfare policies to change the length of time recipients can remain on the roles. They are also revamping policies to reflect changes in job training, work programs, and daycare options, but there is still a long way to go to make a real difference in the average welfare parent's ability to break out of the system. Meanwhile, employed parents who have been able to avoid public assistance must hand over half their take-home pay to daycare providers, or else settle for substandard care for their children.

Single parents usually don't have the luxury of quitting their jobs to retrain for new careers or try their hands at self-employment. They often feel stuck, and resign themselves to maintaining the status quo, at least until the children are grown. No wonder I hear so many single mothers talk about finding a Prince Charming to save them. It's not that they really want a man to fix their problems; it's just that they see little hope for a future in the competitive, and often male-oriented, workplace.

After I received a degree from a two-year college, I transferred to a four-year institution to pursue my bachelor's degree. The four-year university, however, was twice as expensive as the community college. I inquired about financial aid and grants, but was told I made too much money. I laughed. As I saw it, I was barely putting food on the table. I couldn't believe it. I was in an income bracket where Uncle Sam was willing to give me Earned Income Credit at tax time (any head of household making under a specified amount per year is eligible), yet it was too much income to justify receiving financial grants to help pay for my college tuition. My employer certainly was not going to be sympathetic enough to raise my salary, and quitting my job would be a threat to my child's welfare. I was, in a word, stuck.

I spent about a year saving money and put enough away to feel comfortable going from full-time to part-time employment so that I could qualify for financial aid and still make ends meet. It was amazing how much the government would do for me when I put the health and welfare of my kids in jeopardy. I quit my full-time job, considerably reducing my income, gave up all financial security, and voila! I was issued a government grant and a student loan to make it work. Later, I was able to finish my education with merit scholarships, but I needed the initial financial boost so I could get my foot in the door to prove my worthiness.

I'm not suggesting others should do as I did. I tell this story merely to point out the backward nature of the system. There's no doubt: our government's educational policies for single parents leave a lot to be desired. Nevertheless, anyone can achieve his or her career dream, regardless of the sobering statistics or lack of social awareness and interest. It takes determination and hard work, but it can be done.

No Excuses

I've talked with hundreds of women over the years who seem to think they are incapable of learning and succeeding at anything new. Somewhere along the line, they've been told by parents, spouses, or friends that getting ahead was reserved for the lucky ones. I suspect the naysayers in their lives discouraged them for one of two reasons: (1) misery loves company, or (2) the realization that responsibility is a personal choice just might make them accountable for their own lives. Whatever the reason, it's hogwash (that's a midwestern term).

Most people are naturally opposed to learning new things because of fear of failure. "What if I don't do well and end up looking stupid?" "What if I'm not smart enough?" "What if my brain isn't large enough to hold another bit of information?" To answer these questions, I offer the following:

- Making an effort to do something more challenging is always going to be respected by the people in your life who really count. Ignore the others.
- No one is asking you to become a nuclear scientist or brain surgeon, unless, of course, you feel drawn to those professions, which is exactly the point. We usually feel attracted to areas and levels of skill that are within our comfort zones. Trust your instincts. Know the difference between lack of ability and lack of desire. If the desire is strong enough, chances are you have the intelligence to back it up.
- Folk wisdom says that we use about 10 percent of our brain's total capacity. It might sound like a good excuse, but you've got a long way to go before your mental hard drive crashes!

There is absolutely no good reason to believe that learning new skills and succeeding in life is beyond your reach. The next hurdles are a little tougher than merely deciding whether you're capable or not. Identifying the why, what, how, and when of changing your career takes time, effort, and a degree of resourcefulness. The why and when will be answered as you take personal inventory of your life as we discussed in chapters 1–3. Everyone will have different reasons for making career changes, ranging from needing financial stability to desiring a greater sense of self-worth or life fulfillment. Timing will depend on a variety of individual circumstances and maturity levels. In this chapter, therefore, we focus primarily on the questions of what and how.

It's All Up to You

For most people, deciding what to do in life is a pretty tough decision, and one that requires more than a few moments' thought. Maybe that's why so many of us avoid thinking about it. Besides, when we simply react to life as it presents itself, we can make *life* itself responsible for what happens to us, rather than taking any responsibility ourselves. How many times have you heard the following statements?

"I'd be able to afford a nicer car if my boss would give me a raise."

"The factory laid me off, so the bank foreclosed on my house."

"She got the promotion because she's always kissing up."

"It's not *what* you know, but *who* you know."

"They hired a snot-nosed kid right out of college to be my boss."

These seemingly good excuses often elicit a sympathetic response, but if you examine them closely you will find that they contain a common thread: everything is someone else's fault. Before you can identify the need and desire to make a change, it's imperative that you get past the blaming stage. Just as we discussed in chapter 3, blaming keeps you in the past.

No matter how much you believe in your excuses, you simply cannot deny that your success depends on the choices you make. You may have a tougher time than others because of barriers beyond your control (race, gender, age, and so on), but probably your toughest obstacle is the one you've created for yourself by failing to believe in your potential. To overcome this obstacle, you've got to allow yourself the luxury of dreaming. If you've been struggling for some time, it might be tough to begin this process, but it's free and can be a lot of fun.

Once you've decided you need to make a career change, ask yourself a few simple questions in order to reveal the what. We'll call these the "I" questions:

1. Am I happy in my current job?

    —If so, how could I enhance my skills to make it more enjoyable or profitable?

—If not, what is it I don't like—hours, pay, people, tasks?

2. If I could walk into any job tomorrow (no questions asked), where would I choose to go? Why?

3. If I were financially independent, what would I do with my time?

4. If money were no object, what would I do to improve myself personally, academically, or socially?

5. What profession or activity did I secretly dream about as a child?

Sometimes, by asking these kinds of questions, we unlock hidden desires we didn't realize were there. Some people have never thought about these things because they've always discounted their ability to ever achieve them. Many were raised with strong opposition to dreaming:

"Don't get your hopes up and you won't be disappointed."

"No use thinking about something you can't have."

"There's no time to waste on foolish notions."

This so-called sensible philosophy can breed a stable no-nonsense approach to life, but it can also block valuable forethought and necessary planning for today's complicated and competitive environment. By allowing yourself to think beyond the present, you may discover that your current situation isn't as sensible and practical as you once thought.

For example, Linda has been working as a factory supervisor for the past seven years. Linda is thankful for her job, but it's not something she ever dreamed she'd be doing at this stage in her life. When her husband divorced her unexpectedly two years ago, she was left with three children to feed and a house to pay for. She always thought of her job as a second income, extra money to help pay for things like a nicer car, a yearly vacation, and her daughter's orthodontics. When it became her sole income, however, her job no longer looked very appealing. Nevertheless, after seven years, Linda thought it made sense to continue on until her retirement was vested in three more years.

When Linda was asked about her desire to do something different with her life, her response was, "I don't know. It would be nice to not work these crazy hours . . . you know, to have more time to be a real mom. Things get so crazy around our house now that their father isn't around anymore. It doesn't feel like we're a family. I'm just maintaining a lifestyle." Therein lay Linda's why. Deep down she wanted more than the good pay she was receiving. Upon further inspection, Linda discovered she felt no pride in her work. To her, it was work anybody could do. She knew she was intelligent and outgoing, and she could probably use her people skills in a job that would make her feel more fulfilled. It became apparent that Linda wanted more than a better work schedule; she wanted to feel pride not only in her career but in her ability to handle job and motherhood simultaneously, with satisfaction.

I once asked a friend, who was also contemplating a career change, to write down her idea of a perfect day. Here's what she wrote:

I wake up in the morning before my kids get out of bed. I make a cup of coffee and scan the newspaper. I greet each of my kids one by one as they make their sleepy-eyed way into the kitchen. We chat for a few minutes over a piece of toast or bowl of cereal. I go shower and pick out what I'm going to wear for the day. I dress, put finishing touches on my hair and face, and the three of us are out the door to start our day. I'm not in a big hurry, but fully aware of the necessary routine while looking forward to the challenges.

After dropping the kids off at school, I make my way to work. I arrive early enough to stop and talk with a few of my co-workers and to grab another cup of coffee while it's fresh. Whatever job I'm doing, I know it well and feel confident about my ability to do it. My superiors and my peers respect me because of my knowledge and my commitment to hard work. I want to be there because it feels good to be appreciated—it feels good to be paid for work I enjoy—it feels good to be challenged, knowing I can handle whatever problems confront me. At the end of the day, I'm tired, but not exhausted. I look forward to picking up my kids and hearing about their days. They help me with dinner; I help them with homework. We laugh and share stories before bed. I hear their prayers, then I say my own. I'm thankful for what I have. I'm not materially rich, but I'm spiritually and personally fulfilled. Life isn't perfect, but it's meaningful.

My friend's idea of a perfect day may be completely different from what you might want. Again, what's important is your ability to picture the kind of daily routine that would be comfortable for you and your family. Obviously, my friend's day sounds like something from a modern-day storybook. She doesn't mention the kids grumbling about helping with dinner or fighting with each other over the last bit of Frosted Flakes. But just because we know life is never perfect doesn't mean we shouldn't think about the ideal. Carl Shurz said, "Ideals are like stars: you will not succeed in touching them with your hands, but you choose them as your guides."

It's easy to dream, but it's much tougher to make all the pieces of the career puzzle fit. Many things have to be considered, such as your personality and temperament, your likes and dislikes, current job availability, compensation, geographic location, and required education or training. These must all be resolved one by one before you can realistically start on a road to learning new skills.

Step #1
Dig deep to the bottom of your desires.

- Answer the "I" questions.
- Study your answers and look for a common theme.
- Write a paragraph about what you think a perfect day would be like.

Self-Analysis

Who Am I?

If you've never had your personality analyzed or taken a personality test, this might be a great place to begin. Personality profiles can be a mirror for us, revealing our true selves, sometimes even reflecting things about us we don't necessarily want to face. They can help us understand who we are and how we interact with other personality styles or types. There are a number of these profiles and tests:

- Myers-Briggs Type Indicator (also known as the MBTI): Based on Jungian theory, this analysis of style lists sixteen different types based on four areas: introversion/extroversion, intuition/sensation, thinking/feeling, and judging/perceiving. Scores from a lengthy questionnaire point to one of sixteen possible combination types.
- Berkeley Personality Profile: Individual profiles are based on five dimensions of style: expressive, interpersonal, work, emotional, and intellectual. Scores

from several questionnaires are described in degrees along a continuum.

- Lüscher Color Test: This color selection test is used primarily by psychology professionals to better understand a client's characteristics and motivations. Five areas are analyzed: desired objectives, existing mood, characteristics under restraint, suppressed characteristics, and stress behavior.
- Riso Enneagram Type Indicator: Each subject, based on his or her answers to 144 questions, is categorized into one of nine different types: reformer, helper, motivator, artist, thinker, loyalist, generalist, leader, and peacemaker.

Although the MBTI seems to be the most popular these days, the Berkeley Personality Profile is the most useful because it analyzes how subjects see themselves, how they would like to see themselves, and how others, including close friends, family members, and coworkers, see them. This profile helps people understand themselves more deeply, as opposed to the MBTI or Enneagram way of typecasting subjects into categories by generalizing a person's behavior in the past, disregarding roles, and so on. The Berkeley profile doesn't hand out labels (something we've all got plenty of), but rather it considers who people are in different situations (at home, at work, with close friends, with strangers). As a result, subjects are better able to see a well-rounded picture of a unique individual, not a textbook clone. The Lüscher test is quick and fun, but is meant for a deeper analysis of present mood and self-diagnosis of problem behavior. Use of this test should be limited to a professional who knows how to interpret its significance.

No matter how it is attained, a keener sense of self will help you decide in what capacity you will be most comfortable working. It will also give you insight into the behaviors and actions of those around you. For example, if you've always been criticized by your family or friends for being shy or distant, you may discover through reading more about personality types and styles that you're not impaired but just have a unique style of relating to others. You may also discover that many other people like you are successful and have been able to use their quiet nature to their benefit. If you are the quiet type, it stands to reason that a job selling life insurance may not be the best choice for you. Similarly, a person with a gregarious style might feel like a caged animal as a computer programmer. Knowing yourself, and learning to be proud of who you are, will help you in your quest to learn new skills.

What Do I Like?

When I first went back to college, I planned on pursuing a business management degree, not so much because I loved business, but because my employer at the time offered to pay for business-related classes. Sounds like a good deal, but not very smart when I was sleeping through every course. I was energized by my English and philosophy classes, but thought they would never help me get a decent job. It wasn't until I took a computerized career placement test that I discovered I belonged in a more creative field, such as journalism or advertising. Most every college or university admissions office has these tests available free of charge to people who want to embark on a new career but have no idea where to start.

Career placement tests are simple and easy to take. They're somewhat long and involved, but well worth the time and effort. Similar to personality profiles, career placement tests try to get to the bottom of your style, through work-related, multiple-choice questions. After answering a hundred or so questions, the program will give a generalized analysis of the types of jobs you will most likely be happy performing and those you will excel in. It makes sense that if you enjoy what you do, you'll do a better job and be happier doing it. Call your local college or university for more details, or check with your reference librarian for the nearest career placement or occupational interest test center.

Will It Be Worth It?

With any luck, the personality profiles and career placement/occupational interest tests will give you the information you need to make a decision about your career path. The next step is to consider your geographical location and determine whether or not your chosen profession will be profitable where you live. Obviously, if you live in the Southwest and decide you want to be a forest ranger, a move is definitely in order. Sometimes, however, it's not that simple. To avoid spending a lot of time and energy only to be disappointed, it's wise to analyze the local job market. This will help you determine what the demand is for the profession in your area, the average pay scale, and what the forecast for the industry is in the next decade.

Imagine spending years (and money) studying to become a computer analyst only to find out at graduation that there is an overabundance of computer analysts in your area and not much demand. Generally, thanks to the laws of supply and demand, the salary will be low and competition will be high for the good jobs. For many single parents, most of whom lack the option to just pick up and move across the country (because of custody arrangements), such a discovery could be devastating. Don't be foolish. Check out all the facts before you embark on a long, and possibly futile, journey.

Every two years, the Bureau of Labor Statistics (BLS) develops projections of labor force and economic growth, industry output and employment, and occupational employment under three sets of alternative assumptions: low, moderate, and high. These projections cover a ten- to fifteen-year period and provide a framework for the discussion of job outlook for approximately 250 occupations. The bureau prints the projections in a handbook, which identifies the principal factors affecting job prospects, then discusses how these factors are expected to affect each occupation. Your reference librarian can show you how to find and use a copy of the latest BLS handbook.

Also available at most libraries is the *Dictionary of Occupational Titles*, published by the U.S. Employment Service, and the *Encyclopedia of Careers and Vocational Guidance,* published by J. G. Ferguson Publishing. Each of these comprehensive guides can help you determine whether or not your prospective career options are wise choices.

One particularly useful book is the *100 Best Careers for the Year 2000* by Shelly Field. Careers are listed in alphabetic order, with easy-to-read descriptions of each, including potential earnings, recommended education and training, skills and personality traits needed to succeed, and experience and qualifications necessary to break into the field.

Most states have Career Information Delivery Systems (CIDS) in secondary schools, postsecondary institutions, libraries, job training sites, vocational rehabilitation centers, and employment service offices. With CIDS, job seekers can use computers, printed material, microfiche, and toll-free hotlines to obtain information on occupations, educational opportunities, student financial aid, apprenticeships, and military careers. The computerized systems are easy to use, and allow you to search by indicating a profession (or choosing from a coded list) and your place of residence. Printed results contain what you can expect regarding availability, salary, and outlook.

Step #2
Learn about yourself and your options.

• Use a personality profile or test to better understand your style.
• Take a career placement or occupational interest test.
• Investigate demand, salary, and outlook for prospective careers.

Skill Development Possibilities

Once you decide to learn new skills, you will need to look at one of two alternatives:

1. On-the-job training
2. Higher education

On-the-Job Training

Your desire to enhance your job skills may be as simple as looking at your current employment situation and deciding whether or not there are opportunities right where you are. Something initially attracted you to your current job, whether it was the nature of the business or the kind of work you perform. It could simply be that you are no longer feeling challenged in your current position, but challenging opportunities could be available if you ask for them. If your employer has been pleased with your performance, and especially if you've invested more than two years with the company, it may be wise to inquire about current or future opportunities to move up in the company or retrain for another position. Most employers welcome that kind of loyalty and ambition, and may even be willing to create an on-the-job training program especially for you—teaming you with a senior colleague, for example.

Some of the benefits of on-the-job training:

1. Employer-paid programs during regular working hours
2. Experience that may qualify for future college credit
3. Acquired skills that increase a worker's value in the job market, without monetary investment

Kevin has custody of his eight-year-old son and has been working for a large produce distributor since he was fifteen, when he worked after school and during the summers. Kevin, now twenty-seven, has enjoyed continued success on the job and has moved up to a supervisory position. However, Kevin's loyalty to ABC Foods over the past twelve years has not produced the income he would like. His dreams of affording a nicer car and a larger home, in an area with better schools, require a higher salary. Additionally, Kevin has aspirations of running the company someday.

Kevin realizes ABC Foods is a small, family-owned company, and in order to command a higher salary, he needs to continue to improve his position within the organization. He is not willing to look elsewhere for other opportunities because he genuinely likes the company, respects his superiors, and is confident about the work he performs. However, Kevin is apprehensive about the possibilities for the future.

Like Kevin, you may be faced with a situation you are generally happy with, but are seeking more challenges and a brighter future. Unless your company publicizes a variety of training programs (and most do not), you will have to take the first step. To get the ball rolling, make an appointment with your boss (or another superior you feel comfortable talking with), or write him or her a letter describing what you would like to accomplish. Here's an example:

Dear Mr. Smith:

I have been working for ABC Foods for twelve years and have enjoyed my work here so far. I feel I am ready for more interesting and challenging opportunities and would like to know what management training programs are available within the company. As an inventory supervisor, I may have the background needed to go into shipping/receiving management. I would be willing to spend some extra hours after work to accomplish this. Please let me know when we can get together and talk about this further.

Sincerely,

Kevin Jones

There's no need to mention that you are a single parent, life is hard, and you need extra money. Not that they will be insensitive to that, but it will probably be perceived as whining or a plea for special treatment. Your letter (or conversation) should be short and to the point, and should include ideas that show you have carefully considered your options.

Chances are, you will receive a response right away; if you inquire personally, you should get a response instantly. If not, be patient. These things may take time, depending on the culture at your place of employment and whether or not moving up is encouraged or discouraged. In the latter case, the best advice is to begin searching for a new employer who is willing to work with you. In the former case, follow these tips:

- Marry your talents with your employer's interests. Assess your strengths and the company's needs and be prepared to outline how you can fill a void in the company.
- Consult mentors. Before putting your proposal in front of the employer, run it by a trusted colleague. He or she can give you valuable feedback that can prevent fatal blunders.
- Put your request in writing. Remember, this was your idea. Your boss will expect you to have a clear-cut plan in mind and will be impressed with your preparedness and level of organization if you leave something in writing.
- During your conversation, be honest about your intentions. Again, keep the focus on your job, not on your personal family life. If you get into the personal aspects too much, your employer might be uncomfortable with giving you more responsibility, for fear you are already overloaded with responsibilities at home.
- Shy away from overkill statements like "This is the greatest company in the world" or "I want the president's job someday," unless, of course, you genuinely feel that way. Although it may be "old school," it still holds true that most supervisors are impressed with employees who display an honest attempt to work hard for their pay. Limited talk, with a lot of action, will go a long way toward furthering your career.
- Be patient, but persistent. It may take time for your idea to make its way through the approval process. If your supervisor is lukewarm about the proposal, find out why and discuss the reasons. You may uncover some areas where you need to improve, or you may simply find that the timing is off.
- Be flexible. Don't be demanding about compensation or job title. Remember, your goal is to learn new skills that will permanently affect

your ability to command a higher salary, a more challenging position, or both. At the same time, don't let your employer take you for granted. Be honest from the beginning about your intentions of wanting more money and opportunity. Approach each subsequent step with the same candor. A responsible boss will appreciate a flexible, yet straightforward, attitude.

If moving ahead with your present employer is not an option, don't rule out on-the-job training opportunities at other companies. The bottom line is, if you enjoy the kind of job you're currently performing, but feel stagnant or unable to improve your position, there is no reason to go on feeling stuck. Seek out opportunities in your field with other employers. Watch your local classified employment ads and consult with employment agencies about the possibilities. You can also conduct your own search by sending out résumés to companies in your industry. Get their names and addresses out of the phone directory or local business directory. Both are available at your neighborhood library. Check the periodicals section at the library, where you will find trade and professional magazines and journals about specific occupations and industries.

Step #3a
Explore on-the-job training possibilities.

- Ask questions about your employer's training programs.
- Come up with a plan for your promotion and pitch it to the boss.
- Anything worthwhile takes time. Be persistent, patient, and flexible.

Higher Education

After analyzing your personality type, career interests, and job market opportunities, you may discover your career goals can only be met by obtaining a certificate or degree through a college or university. This is a more complicated route to take than on-the-job training, because you must find the time and money, outside your present employment, to accomplish your objectives.

Many single parents, especially if they lack self-esteem and have just come through negative circumstances, doubt their ability to return to a school setting.

If you're one of them, remember these three don'ts:

- Don't look at your or other people's past failures to determine your chances for academic success in the future. People and circumstances change. Look ahead.
- Don't avoid returning to school because of economics. There are numerous ways to get an education without going broke, such as grants, loans, and scholarships. Talk with financial counselors at your prospective school.
- Don't avoid college because you haven't been to school for a long time or because of poor high school performance. Life experience has a way of bringing about the maturity that can make a person an excellent student. You are not who you were in high school, and you definitely have different goals now.

Before getting started on the academic trail, there are other variables to consider:

1. Type of Institution

The first order of business is to choose the institution that best suits your needs with regard to location, price, flexibility of study programs, and accreditation in your chosen field. Where you live may limit you to only one or two choices. If you live in a large metropolitan area, or are willing to relocate, you may have a bigger selection to choose from. The *College Blue Book,* updated every two years, is a five-volume set that includes virtually every college and university in the United States. *Lovejoy's College Guide,* also published by Macmillan, is another comprehensive choice. Between the two, you will find all the important statistics you need about enrollment, price, degree programs, and so on. See your reference librarian about this and similar college data books.

After narrowing your search to a few colleges that seem to fit your requirements, call the admissions department of each for a current catalog and information on how to apply. Many large libraries carry microfiche copies of college catalogs that you can access for free. If possible, visit the college to get a better feel for campus life. Be sure to check accreditation on any college or school of higher learning you are considering. You don't want to find out your degree is worthless after investing years of time and a lot of money. There are national, regional, and field-specific accreditation bodies that can help you find the institution that best suits your needs.

2. Type of Degree

The type of certification or degree you decide to pursue will depend on the field you've chosen. As you are researching career opportunities, note the educational requirements listed for each job. One of the best ways to get this information is to call companies in your area who hire people in your desired occupation. Ask them what their requirements are. For example, if you want to be an accountant, call a few CPA firms, large corporate offices, and small businesses to find out what experience is required for an entry-level accounting position. They will probably tell you that a four-year accounting degree is required, plus three to five years of experience in the field.

3. Funding

Many people use lack of funding as an excuse not to seek higher education. But this subject is like many of those we've discussed so far in this book. Where there's a will, there's a way. There are a variety of financial aid possibilities, from scholarships to federal grants, that can help you afford an education. You've got to be resourceful enough to investigate and choose one or more that fits your needs. Here are a few possibilities:

- *Personal funds:* If you have a sizeable nest egg, own a lot of assets, or have an above-average income, you may want to pay your own way, which obviously gives you the luxury of choices in both the public and private systems. Even if you do have the ability to pay, however, you may still be eligible to have a portion of the costs paid through merit scholarships, or you may want to cover some of the expense with low-interest student loans. Don't automatically assume you are ineligible for financial aid until you've talked to college representatives first. You may want to consider attending a lower-cost community college for your initial coursework, then transferring to a four-year institution to complete your degree. Community colleges are generally less expensive than public four-year universities.

- *Student loans:* The Federal Family Education Loan (FFEL) program sponsors three types of loans: Federal Stafford Loans, Federal Parent Loans for Students (PLUS), and Federal Consolidation Loans. These government-guaranteed loans are administered jointly by the U.S. Department of Education and loan guaranty agencies.

There are two types of Federal Stafford Loans: Direct and FFEL-sponsored. The terms and conditions of a Direct Stafford or an FFEL Stafford are similar. The major differences between the two are the source of the loan funds, the application process, and the repayment options. An increasing number of schools are participating in the Direct Loan program. Under this program, the funds for your Stafford Loan come to you directly from the U. S. government. If your school does not participate in direct loans, the funds come from a bank, credit union, or other lender that participates in the FFEL program.

The Federal Stafford Loan program includes both subsidized and unsubsidized loans. For subsidized loans, the government pays the interest while the student is attending school at least half-time and during a six-month grace period after the student graduates or stops taking classes, after which the loan and interest payments are paid by the student. Like subsidized loans, unsubsidized loans don't have to be repaid until six months after the student either graduates or quits going to school at least half-time, but, with subsidized loans, interest payments begin immediately after disbursement.

The Federal PLUS program does not have either of these repayment features, although payments may be deferred under some conditions. PLUS loans enable parents with good credit histories to borrow for the educational expenses of any dependent child who is enrolled in an undergraduate program at least half-time.

Consolidation loans allow a borrower to combine different types of federal student loans to simplify repayment. Both the Direct Loan and FFEL programs offer consolidation loans. Generally, to be eligible for a loan, a student must be a U.S. citizen or an eligible noncitizen (as defined by federal rules), attend an eligible institution at least half-time, and be working toward a degree or certificate.

Another type of loan is the Federal Perkins Loan, which is a low-interest (5 percent) subsidized loan for both undergraduate and graduate students with exceptional financial need. The unique feature of this loan is that the school is the lender, but the loan is made with government funds.

Call 1-800-4-FED-AID (1-800-433-3243) for more information on these and other government student aid programs.

- *Grants:* Grants are monetary awards that do not have to be repaid or earned. The most popular grant is the Federal Pell grant, which is based on financial need. Eligibility is limited to undergraduate students, and less-than-half-time students are eligible. The amount of the Federal Pell grant varies depending on a student's financial resources and the amount it will cost a student to attend school. For undergraduate students with exceptional financial need, the Federal Supplemental Educational Opportunity Grant (SEOG) is available. It also does not have to be paid back. Depending on the college or university you have chosen, there are additional state, local, and private grants available to students. Contact the institution's student financial services office for details on how to apply for grants.

- *Scholarships:* Most scholarships are donated to universities by community organizations, business and professional groups, or private citizens. Scholarships are considered gifts and do not need to be repaid. While they are often awarded to students who earn above-average grades, they may also be awarded on the basis of financial need, extracurricular activities, community service, ethnicity, or religious affiliation. Again, your public library will have a number of books on scholarships, and any student financial services office can provide a list of scholarships available to you.

- *Work-study programs:* Federal Work-Study is a federally funded work program based on a student's financial need. It provides jobs to students who qualify, providing them the opportunity to earn money to help pay for college expenses. Other programs that may be available at your college or university include on-campus student employment, job location and development, and community service. Contact your student financial services office for details.

- *Employer reimbursement:* Many employers today are taking an active role in employee education, encouraging employees to pursue opportunities for higher education by offering reimbursement programs as a job benefit. Talk to your manager or human resources manager to find out what benefits, if any, are available to you. Often, employees will be reimbursed for the costs of courses they have completed with a grade of C or better. This reimbursement may be limited, however, to coursework that the employer feels directly increases the performance and value of employees. For example, an accounting firm may reimburse workers for taking accounting and business classes but may not reimburse them for taking music or art courses. Make sure that you are clear about your employer's guidelines for reimbursement before mapping out your academic plan.

4. Nature of Study

Once you have been accepted into an educational program, identify the types of study or credit alternatives offered at the college and decide which fit your time requirements and study habits. Though they are not widely publicized, nontraditional methods of obtaining college credit go a long way to accommodate difficult schedules, such as those of single parents. Investigating the possibilities is definitely worth your while. When I was trying to figure out how I could get credit without actually having to attend class, I discovered that the local community college, working in conjunction with a nearby U.S. Air Force base, offered students video classes. Students could earn credit by watching videos and taking periodic tests that didn't require formal class time. I especially liked this program because I could watch the videos (about twelve in all) after the kids were in bed at night and complete the regular tests on my lunch hours. The coursework required a base pass and some patience with a not-so-organized staff, but I was able to earn nine semester credits with this method.

Some other non-traditional options to earn college credit follow:

- *Prior Learning Assessment (PLA) programs:* Most colleges and universities now recognize that what adults learn on their own through work experience can be similar to what is being taught in the classroom. Therefore, you may begin your college career with credit by having your work experience assessed upon admission.

- *College Level Examination Program (CLEP):* Similar to PLA programs, the CLEP offers an opportunity for you to "test out" of certain classes because of what you know. If you are gifted in writing English essays, for example, you may be able to take a CLEP test in English in lieu of a required first-year composition class, provided that you score high enough on the test. There are general exams and more specific subject exams. Tests are normally administered three or four times per year.

- *Other proficiency tests:* Many tests are available, including the Advance Placement (AP), which is primarily for high school students; the American College Testing Proficiency Examination Program (ACT-PEP); the Defense Activity for Non-Traditional Educational Support (DANTES); and the Student Occupational Competency Achievement Tests (SOCAT). Some colleges also offer special departmental challenge exams. These vary from school to school.

- *Cable television courses:* Much like the video classes mentioned earlier, cable television courses are offered by some cities in conjunction with local colleges and universities. These are great for single parents because they allow you to watch the instruction in the privacy of your own home and take the exams at a high school or local branch of your college.

- *Computer on-line:* Yet another way to take classes from your home, on-line computer classes even have advantages over video and television courses, such as the ability to converse with an instructor via E-mail or to download course materials as needed. The down side, however, is the expense. Most on-line courses are considerably more expensive than attending courses on campus. For some, though, the convenience far outweighs the expense.

- *Employer seminars:* Don't rule out anything when it comes to earning credit the easy way. If you are required by your employer to attend a seminar, and the subject matter fits in with your college study program, find out if you can get credit for attending the seminar. While on the job, I attended a required four-hour employee management seminar each month for a year. That added up to a total of forty-eight hours of instruction. Since I was seeking a minor in business administration, I inquired about getting college credit for attending the seminars. I submitted written documentation of what was taught in the seminars and obtained a letter from my employer verifying my attendance. The seminars met the requirements for a similar course being taught at the college, and I was awarded credit for a full semester class.

- *Independent study:* Many colleges will give credit for special work done outside the classroom under a professor's guidance. These types of allowances are often governed by strict rules. Some colleges allow students to pursue credit outside the classroom only if the coursework involves a subject that is not currently being taught in the curriculum. For example, if you are a business major and there are no courses offered in international marketing, you may ask to research and write a term paper about the subject in order to earn credits toward your degree. Much of this depends upon the amount of time you anticipate spending on the project and upon the format of the project (term paper, internship, independent reading, and so forth). As a journalism major, I was able to get independent study credit by writing a monthly column for a local magazine under the supervision of one of my instructors.

- *Correspondence/Home-study courses:* There are a number of correspondence schools around the country that offer degree programs in a variety of fields. Some of these are institutions that do nothing else but correspondence work. Others are full-blown universities which offer correspondence study as a limited option in their degree programs. If you choose to go this route, contact the National Home Study Council to check accreditation. To get a free directory of home-study schools, write to NHSC, 1601 18th Street, N.W., Washington, DC 20009.

- *Alternative scheduling:* Many colleges and universities are starting to recognize the importance of offering classes that are convenient for adults with full-time work and parenting responsibilities. For example, the university I attended offered weekend seminar classes that could be attended by busy working people with children. It worked out great for me because I was able to attend classes while my kids were on weekend visits with their father. Check into these possibilities before you complete your course plan.

A final word of warning about earning nontraditional credits: These options may seem easy and convenient for the hungry and tired single parent, but they also require self-motivation, flexibility, and commitment. Learning on video or via any home-study program robs you of the opportunity to ask questions spontaneously, so it can be difficult to learn tough concepts. You also must discipline yourself to watch the videos or read the material and take tests regularly with limited supervision. Placement and proficiency tests require significant prior knowledge of a subject or a lot of independent study before the test is administered. If you are like many who suffer from test anxiety, you may have difficulty passing subjects even though you are very knowledgeable about them. Independent study requires the innovation to design your own course, the initiative to work unsupervised, and the responsibility to report regularly to an instructor. If you normally have trouble disciplining or motivating yourself in other areas of life, non-traditional credits may not be for you. However, contrary to the old saying that you can't teach an old dog new tricks, it is possible to change your usual approach when the goal is important enough. There are several guides to help you make the right choices: *Bear's Guide to Earning College Degrees Non-Traditionally, College Degrees by Mail, The Electronic University, The Oryx Guide to Distance Learning,* and *Adult Learner's Guide to Alternative and External Degree Programs.*

Step #3b
Explore higher education possibilities.

• Closely scrutinize educational institutions before making decisions.
• Check out all financial possibilities; don't let money get in your way.
• Choose the right study plan for you and stick with it.

In a Nutshell

Many people stay where they are personally and professionally because making changes requires commitment and a certain amount of risk-taking. The sheer number of choices overwhelms them, causing them to stay where they are comfortable and the scenery is familiar. Gordon Porter Miller, in his book *Life Choices,* lists the myths indecisive people tend to live by:

• Most good things in life are a result of luck.
• What is going to happen will happen.
• Success is the result of being in the right place at the right time.
• There is little an individual can do about what is happening in the world.
• It is not a good idea to plan too far ahead.
• What happens to me is really up to a larger social order.

Compare these myths with a list of more proactive rules for living:

- Good things most always result from some action you take.
- What happens to me is mostly my own doing.
- Success results from hard work.
- The little guy can fight City Hall effectively.
- You may not be able to see the future, but you affect what it can be.[1]

Decision-making is something that takes practice. The more decisions you make, the easier it becomes. The decision to learn new skills does not come without a lot of forethought and consideration of the risks involved. Miller suggests the following useful guidelines for assessing the risk of committing yourself to a new action. They are designed to force the examination of values and to get you to think realistically before you act.

- Can you afford this action in terms of time, energy, and other resources?
- Is the payoff adequate in terms of the risk you are taking?
- Does the action support your goals and values?
- What problems will this action create in terms of the people you love?
- Are there any predictable changes or uncertainties that might spell disaster if you take this action?

If you can answer these questions positively and without reservation, you are on your way to making career decisions that will be good for you and your family. From here, it's simply a matter of anticipating the struggles, keeping your heart in the right place, and discovering the joys of learning.

Checkpoint

- Have you answered the five "I" questions?
- Can you envision a "perfect day"?
- Have you taken a personality type/style test?
- Have you identified your career likes and dislikes?
- Do job prospects and occupational outlooks coincide with your chosen career goals?
- Have you explored on-the-job training possibilities?
- If you've chosen to pursue higher education,
    have you checked accreditation on prospective schools?
    do you understand what your financial choices are?
    have you investigated the various study plans?
- Have you asked yourself the five risk questions?

If you can answer yes to all these questions, go on to chapter 5.

5

LIVING A GOOD LIFE ON ONE INCOME

Happiness does not consist of getting everything you want but of wanting everything you have.
                                                              —Merle Shain

Less Can Be Better

Though leaving a marriage can be a fearful experience, the relief from stress is often a blessing in disguise, according to Rebecca, a single mother and proclaimed penny-pincher. Her annual income of $18,000 fits the norm for most single parents in her position. However, her ability to maintain a $150,000, six-bedroom Virginia home (which she purchased on her own as a single mom), and to amass almost $10,000 for her son's education and her retirement, is definitely above average. Rebecca describes how her single-parent experience strengthened her commitment to success.

"One of the biggest obstacles in our marriage was how we handled money. I was always thrifty while he was always a spender—a symptom, I later learned, of his obsessive-compulsive behavior. Every time I managed to save money to get ahead, he would get himself deep into debt and I would have to bail him out. This may sound arrogant or naive, but I knew I would be better off without him. I had no reservations about raising my son on my own."

Rebecca's savvy, yet simple, money-management techniques aren't revolutionary, but her determination to do more than make ends meet just might be.

"Family happiness and safety are my highest priorities," she says, "but financial welfare is just as important. In order to be able to have security in life, you must be in control of your money; you can't let it control you."

After her marriage dissolved, Rebecca systematically set financial goals and made commitments to them. "First, I had to decide what my goals were going to be," she remembers. "Then I determined how much money it would take to reach each goal. I set up a working budget, tracked all my expenses, and began investing money every month. To keep it going, I always looked for reasonable ways to cut back."

Rebecca says she's been frugal ever since she got her first job at age sixteen. She saved money to buy her first car, which she is still driving. Later, she had to use her financial resourcefulness to counteract her husband's spending habits. She says proudly, "Now, I use my know-how to maintain our quality of life and invest like crazy."

Teaching her five-year-old son the financial ropes has also been a challenge for Rebecca. She says that giving time and money to her community and church are good teaching tools. "I think he is learning responsibility and to give of himself unselfishly. He is learning that material possessions mean nothing, and that home, family, and friends mean everything."

Rebecca says she's learned to take advantage of free and low-cost activities such as trips to the library, picnics in the park, hiking, craft projects, seasonal fruit picking, fishing, bike riding, cooking, civic activities, and many more.

"I was lucky that my son was only two years old when my husband and I split. He hasn't known any other way of life besides the frugal way. That has made the process a little easier for me than for many parents, whose children have to make a major lifestyle adjustment."

Rebecca's goals include buying land and building her own home, a college education for her son, and early retirement. When asked if she feels confident about attaining these goals, she answers, "Absolutely." Her spending plan is somewhat unconventional, but she says everyone must decide on a system that is custom-fit to his or her personality.

"The system I use may seem complex to some, but it works for me. I have three checking accounts and two savings accounts, all service-charge free. I utilize direct deposit and have different purposes for each account. One checking account is for my son. All his expenses, except housing and food, come out of this fund (daycare, clothes, medical, haircuts, and fun stuff). This way, at a glance, I can tell my son if we can afford to do something or not, and I don't have to worry about spending the car insurance money accidentally.

"The second checking account is for all my housing expenses: mortgage, utilities, and all repairs. The third checking account is for all my living expenses: clothing, food, insurance. I have one savings account that is for emergencies and bills I pay annually (like car insurance). It gets a higher rate of interest. The other savings account is for small vacations. I put only miscellaneous income, such as from baby-sitting and yard sales, into it.

"Finally, I take maximum advantage of my employer's 401(k) plan. I also use the medical and daycare tax shelters. I have an automatic withdrawal every month for my Individual Retirement Account (IRA) and my son's college fund. I invest a little over 30 percent of my income and give 10 percent to the church. I am able to live off of 60 percent of what I make."

Rebecca's advice for single parents facing tight financial circumstances is simple and straightforward: "Pay off debt, be as frugal as possible, and spend every spare moment at the library.

"Forget the 'if onlys' and take a good look in the mirror. You must take care of you and your family. And you can do it!"

❀❀❀❀❀❀❀❀❀

George Bernard Shaw said, "To the person with a toothache, even if the world is tottering, there is nothing more important than a visit to a dentist." I love this quote because, as much as we don't like to think about the subject of money, it is all we can think about when we don't have enough of it. A large percentage of the single-parent population can barely make ends meet. The painful truth is that many parents have such a tough time dealing with the job and money issues that child-rearing becomes a secondary concern.

In the last chapter, you learned some ways to build a career and increase your earning power. While you're working toward your financial goals, however, you don't have to be financially miserable. In fact, there are numerous ways to positively affect your financial status. In a very short period of time, you and your children could afford a healthy and happy lifestyle, regardless of your career choice. As we go through these ideas and suggestions, keep one thing in mind: The best things in life are free.

Taking Inventory of What You Have

Like many soon-to-be-single parents, the divorce process catapulted me into a state of self-preservation. I felt I had to fight for my rights, to go after everything I deserved. "After all he put me through, I should get something to show for it," I thought. I fought because I was in pain, and somehow fighting for material things helped validate my desire to win the divorce game.

Looking back, I now realize that my children and I could have walked away from everything without the promise of child support or financial security, and I would have found a way to keep a roof over our heads and food on the table. That doesn't mean I shouldn't have exercised our rights, but I know now that money played an insignificant role in our happiness. In fact, what I had in me and in my relationship with the children was all I needed for personal fulfillment. Once I heard a minister say that when all you have left is the grace of God, that's when you discover that God's grace is all you really need. Needing nothing more than you have is a wonderful, liberating feeling. It means you possess a self-sustaining spirit and love that can't be stripped away by divorce, job loss, bankruptcy, or any other material hardship.

Before you embark on this new journey toward making sense of your financial picture, you need to reconcile your personal and material inventory (no matter how meager) with your priorities. You've got to identify the debits and credits in your life, concerning both money and values, and come to a conclusion about your present financial state and where you would like to be in the future. First, take a minute to assess your financial assets and liabilities by completing Worksheets A and B in the Appendix. We'll call these financial assets and liabilities your tangibles. Once you know your financial worth, you will be better equipped to adjust your spending and saving habits.

Next, use Worksheet C in the Appendix to look at those assets and liabilities that can't be calculated in numbers—your intangibles. Intangibles include such assets as your children, friends, religious beliefs, positive personality traits, talents, hobbies, and so on. These assets make up a treasure of emotional, spiritual, and even material wealth that contributes to your ability to be content with what you already possess. Your intangibles can also include liabilities, such as working too much, worrying too much, or spending too much. Whatever your intangibles are, it's a good idea to recognize their roles in adding to or subtracting from your happiness.

Step #1
Determine your personal and financial worth.

• Complete the financial worksheet to assess tangible wealth.
• Complete the spending habits analysis to determine areas of change.
• Create a balance sheet to put intangibles in perspective.

Going from Red to Black

Successful money management isn't a skill; it's a lifestyle. There will be fads and get-rich-quick schemes, just like dieting crazes that claim you can lose weight by eating fruit and tofu every other day. But the only way to realize long-lasting change is through a commitment to smart spending habits (cutting out the daily fat) and aggressive saving (regular exercise).

Many people quit listening as soon as they hear the words saving, investment, and budget. "How can I save money when I can't even pay my bills every month?" is the most common response. "Investing? That's only for the rich," might be another. And let's face it, budgeting is about as exciting a word as dieting. They both suggest that we've got to sacrifice something. Regardless of your preconceived notions about these concepts, they still constitute the basics of good money management. This chapter will reduce them to digestible portions by introducing a spending plan that is simple, wise, and flexible; a savings goal that reflects newly discovered money sources; and an investment strategy you can understand.

Staying Ahead of the Game by Avoiding Risk

There are several ways to organize your financial affairs to ensure that expenses are planned for and bills get paid regularly. Most financial plans require a detailed and complicated income/expense analysis coupled with a budget proposal almost no one can stick with. The plan I'm going to share with you is not based on any scientific or mathematical theories, just life experience. You might choose to create your own variation on my method, but whatever you decide, you must have a plan. The "pay as you go" philosophy won't net anything but stress and regret. The following plan is what I call the Simple Allocation Method. You will need

- a checking account
- a notebook (or personal computer if you have one)
- about thirty minutes per week

The first step is to complete the income/expense worksheet in the Appendix (Worksheet D). Take some time to list your actual expenses (use your checkbook or receipts to get an accurate total). Next, multiply your total net income by the percentages listed next to each expense area. These percentages are given only as a guideline to help you identify areas that may be lopsided, so that you can realign your goals to reflect more flexibility and balance in your total financial picture. Obviously, you can determine your own percentages in accordance with your objectives and priorities.

Compare your actual numbers with the target figures. Understandably, there will be areas that cannot be changed in the short term without making major adjustments. If you have substantial credit card debt or other expenses that can't be adjusted right away, you'll have to tough it out for a while before you can bring more balance to your situation. The idea behind allocating funds is not to set limits on what you spend your money on, as much as it is to make sense of how you justify your expenditures.

Donna is a single parent of two children, ages six and four. She works as a secretary making $2,000 per month (her net is $1,600 after taxes and a minimal medical insurance deduction). She receives $400 in monthly child support. She rents a three-bedroom home. Let's look at a summary of Donna's worksheet:

Net Income	$1,600	(salary)
	<u>400</u>	(child support)
Total Net Income	$2,000	

	Actual	Goal	
Home Expenses	600	600	(30%)
Utilities	225	200	(10%)
Daycare	410	300	(15%)
Food & Personal Items	325	300	(15%)
Transportation	400	200	(10%)
Savings/Investments	0	200	(10%)
Other	<u>40</u>	<u>200</u>	<u>(10%)</u>
Total Expenses	$2,000	$2,000	(100%)

Donna has calculated her new goals in the right-hand column using the percentages suggested on the worksheet. In order to free up money to meet her new goals, Donna decides to sell the new car she bought last year that has a high loan payment and expensive insurance costs. She can buy a used car, cutting her loan and insurance expenses by half. She also decides she can spend less on utilities (by making fewer long-distance phone calls) and on food and personal items. In addition, Donna's four-year-old daughter will be entering kindergarten in the fall, which will cut her daycare expenses by $110 a month. These adjustments will give Donna more flexibility in the areas of savings and other expenses.

The next step is to determine which portion of your income is reliable and which portion might be at risk. Donna has determined that her child support income is at risk because her ex-husband has a history of frequent job changes. If he loses his job or takes a job earning much less, her child support income could disappear or be drastically reduced. Since Donna has no funds currently allocated for savings, she could find herself in a tight situation if she should lose her child support income. Therefore, Donna decides to allocate the money from child support to accounts she can live without—savings and other expenses.

Another form of income Donna considers at risk is the occasional overtime pay she receives (approximately $100 extra per month). She chooses not to include this in her net income because it is sporadic, but it does provide her with extra padding in her checking account.

Donna decides to allocate her income as follows:

1. Child support ($400)
   - $200 to be immediately deposited in her savings account (a portion could be deducted each month for an investment plan)
   - $200 in cash to be put in an envelope or jar at home for lunches, entertainment, clothing, kids' allowances, and unexpected needs for the month
2. Employment ($1,600)
   - Total to be deposited in checking account to pay bills

With this new allocation plan, Donna will be protected in the event that her child support income stops or is reduced. In addition, she knows when the cash in the jar at home is gone, she must stop spending until the next check comes. The money jar will serve as a concrete reminder to Donna to spend wisely and at a reasonable pace. Finally, she can feel comfortable knowing there is enough money in her checking account to pay the bills. If she finds she is going to run short for some reason, she has the option of taking money from the cash jar or working overtime to make up the difference. Meanwhile, she is building a savings account for the future. Other ideas for frugal spending, particularly in emergencies, are listed in the next section.

If, for whatever reason, you prefer not to have a checking account, this method can still be effective. In Donna's case, she could cash her entire paycheck and divide the money into envelopes, each marked with the names and amounts for her accounts (rent/$500, car payment/$187, daycare/$300, and so forth). It may take more discipline and self-control with this method to keep from robbing cash from the envelopes when you need something. You might try leaving IOUs to yourself or take small amounts from a flexible account like groceries. When using cash, it's best to pay bills soon after you get paid to avoid temptation.

Five Keys to Staying out of Debt

1. Anticipate problems. When it rains, it pours, the old saying goes, and it happens to the best of us. Make a list of problems that could hinder your ability to live, work, or eat: car breakdown, refrigerator blowup, sewage problem, and so on. Would you know what to do in these situations? Who would you call? Where would you find low-cost services or merchandise?

2. Call your church or synagogue. Find out if there is a list of church members who have special skills and are willing to share them for a reasonable price with other members in need. Many churches have directories listing members' occupations and office numbers.

3. Check the classifieds. When something does go awry, check the local paper for items like cars and home appliances before resorting to department store "no interest, no payment for a bazillion years" gimmicks. Although some finance plans seem convenient now, you'll have to pay sometime. If at all possible, pay cash.

4. Ask for help from friends and family. Many times they have resources and contacts that can help solve your problem with minimum cash outlay.

5. Wait. I call it the two-day delay. Before making any credit purchase, even if it seems like an emergency, take two days to think about possible alternatives and about whether or not the purchase makes sense financially. Talk to a friend or family member about it first. If it still feels right two days later, it's probably a good decision.

Step #2
Make decisions based on valid and reliable facts.

- Distinguish reliable from at-risk income.
- Adjust expenses so that at-risk"income can be allocated to nonessential accounts.
- Be flexible, allowing for fluctuations, and have fun!

Discovering a Pot of Gold

The wise old suggestions that we should save 10 percent and give 10 percent of our income are admirable goals, but nearly impossible for many single parents. Single mothers are the least likely group to save or donate because 36 percent of them earn less than $10,000 per year (that's below the poverty level). In fact, 79 percent of all single mothers in the United States earn less than $30,000 per year. With rising costs of housing, daycare, and food and clothing essentials, a savings plan is only a dream for many of these families.

There are ways to rise above these statistics and develop a comfortable savings plan, of course. But before you can begin to think about savings, you must be able to get your hands on extra money. Donna was able to find extra dollars for savings by cutting transportation and daycare costs. It's not always that clear-cut, however; in fact, you may already be operating on what you think is the bare bone minimum. Before giving up on the idea of a savings plan, read through the following steps. You may be surprised to find a few extra dollars after instituting these suggestions.

1. Teamwork. Get your kids together and let them know what you are doing. Cut out a picture of the goal—a college education, a car, a home, a charitable donation—and hang the picture on the refrigerator to remind everyone to be more money-conscious. Then make a list of the ways you are going to cut spending. Keep a journal and make an entry every time you are successful. Don't worry about doing anything with this extra savings for at least sixty days so you can concentrate on developing new habits.

2. Groceries. Spend one to two hours per week planning. Do it first thing Saturday morning after breakfast, or if you're a night owl like I am, do it after the kids go to bed and you have time to concentrate. Look through your grocery store's sale paper for the week and plan your menus accordingly. Plan seven days' worth of menus—everything from the beverage to the salad. Only include planned menu items on your grocery list and buy only what's on your list. Use coupons and stay away from brand-name products. Nine times out of ten, they're no better than the store or generic brand.

   Avoid buying a lot of cleaning products, which really drive up the price of your total grocery bill. A box of baking soda (check the box for handy ways to clean with it), a canister of Comet cleanser, an all-purpose window cleaner, and a bottle of bleach are all you really need for basic housecleaning chores. Baking soda is a good general cleaner; Comet takes care of tougher jobs like the toilet bowl and shower; and window cleaner is useful to shine almost any surface. One part bleach to nine parts water makes the most effective disinfectant around. Contrary to commercial sales pitches, you really don't need a different type of cleaner for every room in your house.

Don't buy personal items (shampoo, razors, toothpaste) at the grocery store. Wait until you can get to a discount department store like Wal-Mart or Target for these items. You'll save 10 to 20 percent, which is worth going out of your way a few extra miles. Plan to save $20 to $40 per week by being grocery-smart.

3. Phone calls. Cut down on long-distance calls. Take turns or alternate phone calls with relatives. Also, analyze your phone bill. Make sure you don't have anything on it you don't need. If you're paying for three-way conferencing and have never used it, cancel it.

4. Gasoline. Find someone at work or in your neighborhood who is willing to carpool. You could save $5 to $10 per week in automobile expenses by doing this. Take advantage of public transportation if it is convenient and will save you money.

5. TV. If you have cable TV, consider canceling it. It's expensive (about $30 per month for basic service) and it doesn't offer much more variety suitable for kids than free TV. Public television (PBS) provides plenty of mind-expanding programming for you and your kids.

6. Postage. Pay bills in person whenever possible. At $0.32 per stamp, you could save $5 or $6 a month bypassing the U.S. Postal Service. Check your local bank or grocery store. Many of them accept electric, gas, phone, and water bill payments.

7. Checking account charges. Find a bank that offers free checking. This could save you $10 to $15 per month in service and check charges.

8. Insurance. Find an insurance expert you trust and ask him or her to help you analyze your car, home, and life insurance. It's possible you are

overpaying for unnecessary coverage.

9. Subscriptions. Don't renew magazine subscriptions. Most magazines can be found at the library. If you can't find time to go to the library, you probably don't have time to read the magazines you're receiving anyway. Stop memberships to book clubs, music clubs, or computer services you don't need.

10. Preventative maintenance. Visit the dentist regularly, change the oil in your car every 3,000 miles, and tuck away credit cards in an inconvenient place. Prevention is always the best medicine for an ailing budget.

Did You Know?

- Dining out for lunch instead of dinner can cost up to $10 less.
- Taking coffee in a thermos instead of buying it at work can save you $2.75 a week.
- By making your own windshield cleaner fluid with one part ammonia to two parts water, instead of buying ready-made fluid, you'll save $1.80 per one and a half gallons.
- Increasing the thermostat setting from seventy-eight degrees to eighty degrees can save about 11 percent on your air-conditioning bill.
- Lowering your water heater's thermostat to 120 degrees can save up to 10 percent on your utility bill.
- A brown-bag lunch costs about 60 percent less than eating out.
- Hanging your wash outdoors instead of using a dryer can save $1.39 every three loads.
- Hair cuts, washes, styles, and perms cost about half as much at beauty-school salons than they do at professional salons.
- You'll save $1 for every three days you don't run that extra refrigerator or freezer in the garage.

Besides conserving to save money, you might consider ways to make money by renting

- a room or computer time to a college student

- practice time on your piano
- garage space
- storage space in your basement or attic
- lawn mower or other yard equipment
- washer or dryer
- freezer space

You can also turn a profit by

- having a garage or yard sale
- selling clothing, baby equipment, and toys to consignment shops
- marketing your skills in cleaning, home or car maintenance, baking, ironing, woodworking, or child care

Uncle Sam is also a good source of income if you've been lending the government money every paycheck and getting it back in the form of a refund every year. Your payroll department can help you complete a W-4 form, a worksheet for calculating how many exemptions you're entitled to. Increasing your exemptions will give you more money each payday to save and earn interest. Don't use the government's 0 percent interest plan as a savings tool; your local bank can do better than that. You may discover an extra $10 per week this way, which could grow to $10,000 over ten years in an investment earning 12 percent.

Step #3
Find treasure in hidden places.

- Make good saving habits a family project.
- Cut back on unnecessary waste, luxuries, and conveniences.
- Discover new ways to increase income with a little investment of time.

Making Dreams Come True

After a sixty-day period, take a few minutes to look at your savings journal to determine the amount you can comfortably put aside for savings and investments. Don't be surprised if it adds up to $100 or more. Warning: You probably won't find an extra $100 bill in your wallet at this point, but you have now proved to yourself that you can come up with extra money to save.

The next and most important steps are to devise methods of saving the new-found money to achieve your long-term goals.

1. Save half in an easily accessible account (credit union, bank savings account, and so forth) for your emergency fund. Have this money deducted directly from your paycheck or checking account. Do this until the balance reaches the equivalent of two months' take-home pay. Then you can begin to apply this half to your long-term investments.

2. Save the other half in a mutual fund or other long-term investment account. This money should only be used for long-term goals such as college, retirement, home purchase, new car, and so on. Once you start, don't look back. The rewards will be well worth the sacrifice, both in peace of mind and self-esteem.

Using Donna's example, let's see what she could do with her allocated savings amount:

$200 ——▶ Deposited in bank savings account
(100)——▶ Mutual fund company drafts from the account monthly
$100 ——▶ Stays in local account

After about three years, Donna will have a good cash reserve in her savings account as an emergency backup, and she will begin to see significant growth in her mutual fund. At that point she could increase the amount for long-term investments or she could begin saving for something special (new furniture, vacation, wardrobe) Invariably, emergencies will present themselves before three years have passed, but the point is, Donna has a plan and clear-cut goals to make her money work for her.

Regular passbook savings at your bank or credit union are simple to open and maintain, but they don't have a lot to offer by way of long-term appreciation. That's why it's wise to invest money where you'll get a greater return over the long haul. This can be a little more complicated, though, and requires some research and asking questions about an intimidating subject. I suspect this is why most people often don't bother to delve into the maze known as the investment world.

Dr. Jagdish Mehta, a finance professor at the University of Nevada-Las Vegas and volunteer financial consultant to single parents, says anyone with $40 to $50 a month to spare can do well investing with very little knowledge about banking or the stock market.

"The key is in finding no-load [no sales commission] mutual funds with stable and reliable companies," said Mehta. "Investors in these conservative funds can earn 15 percent per year, on the average. That's so much better than 2.5 to 3 percent at a bank, and definitely better than not saving at all."

A mutual fund is an investment company that pools the money of thousands of investors to buy a broad selection of stocks, bonds, and other securities. The benefits are instant diversification (your money isn't in jeopardy if one of the stocks takes a nosedive) and the luxury of having experts manage the fund. You just contribute the money and they do the rest. If you choose a no-load (non-commission) fund, you'll end up paying only a modest management fee annually—usually less than 1 percent of your investment.

Two highly recommended no-load funds are 20th Century Funds (1-800-345-2021) and T. Rowe Price Funds (1-800-638-5660). Many mutual funds require an initial investment of $1,000 or more, but at least thirty fund families, including these two, will waive these minimums if you agree to invest $50 to $100 each month (deducted automatically from your checking account).

If you're blurry-eyed looking at the stock page of mutual funds, pick up a few money magazines that will help you decide which funds are best for you. Magazines such as *Money, Smart Money,* and *Fortune* do a good job of relaying information in layman's terms and will recommend different types of funds based on desired levels of risk. In addition, *Consumer Reports* recommends the best mutual funds to buy in a special, annual investment issue. Three of the most conservative types of mutual funds are as follows:

- Blue-chip funds, which consist of well-established company stocks such as McDonalds or General Electric. They generally earn about 8 to 10 percent. Neuberger & Berman Focus (1-800-877-9700) is a good choice in this category with a $50-per-month minimum investment.
- Funds that invest in mid-size firms consist of company stocks that have passed through the high-risk stage of development but are below blue-chip status. These funds are less risky than blue-chip funds, but do approximately

2 percent better on the average. T. Rowe Price Mid-Cap Growth is a good choice in this category with a $50 minimum monthly investment.

- Small company stock funds are ideal for long-term savings plans. Good fund managers buy these companies' stocks at bargain prices and watch them grow over time into solid investments. These funds have delivered average annual returns of 12 percent over the last forty years. Check out Founders Discovery (1-800-525-2440), which has a $50 minimum monthly investment.

Taxes will affect your investment returns in some cases, so it's a good idea to utilize employer 401(k) plans and IRAs to minimize your tax liability on funds earmarked for retirement. Taxes on all earnings in such plans are deferred until you withdraw the money after the age of fifty-nine and a half. In most cases, taxes are deferred on money put into retirement plans, too, so you get an immediate return in the form of a lower tax bill. Talk to a tax professional for more details.

If you're specifically saving for your children's college days, investing in U.S. Series EE savings bonds might be wise. Interest earned on these bonds bought after January 1990 can be totally tax-free if the following requirements are met:

- Bonds are registered in the name of one or both parents (not a child or grandparent) or in the name of an adult who will use them to pay for his or her own education.
- The parent or adult student-to-be was at least twenty-four years old at the time the bonds were purchased.
- The bonds are redeemed to pay tuition and fees for higher education (for the adult bond owner, his or her child, or any other dependent).
- The bonds are redeemed in the year the tuition is due.
- The parents' income does not exceed the maximum in the year the bonds are used (consult a tax professional for the maximum amounts).

Some employers offer a savings bond payroll deduction plan, which is the simplest way to buy them. If not, contact your bank, savings and loan association, or credit union (the U.S. Treasury Department does not sell them directly). Series EE bonds are earning anywhere from 4 to 7.5 percent per year, in addition to the tax savings realized, which will depend on your tax bracket at the time of redemption. For more information, send a postcard to the Bureau of Public Debt, Savings Bond Operations Office, Parkersburg, WV 26106. Ask for the investor information booklet.

If you're still not sold on long-term investing, consider the following (assuming an average return of 12 percent):

- If you start saving $10 per week at age twenty-five, you could have $520,506 at age sixty-five. Saving $10 per week starting at age thirty-five will net you $153,957 in thirty years.

- Depositing $10,000 in a passbook savings account at your bank will take thirty years to double. That same investment in a conservative mutual fund will double in a third of the time, or ten years!

Step #4
Make your newfound earnings work for you.

- Save half of the amount in an accessible account; the other half in long-term investments.
- Know what you're saving for to determine the best investment plan.
- Gather information and get started on a regular investment schedule.

In a Nutshell

Being happy with what you have isn't about ignoring financial issues. Rather, it's about practicing good stewardship with all your assets, both material and personal. In a well-known biblical parable, a man entrusts eight talents (a measure of currency worth more than $1,000 each) to his three servants while he is away on a journey. He gives one servant five talents, another two, and the last only one. Upon returning from his journey, he discovers that the first two servants put their talents to work and each doubled their money. The third servant, being afraid, buried his in the ground to keep it safe. The man was pleased with the two who had doubled their money, and said to both, "You have been faithful with a few things. I will put you in charge of many things." However, he ordered that the talent be taken away from the third servant and that he be thrown out into the darkness.

There is more to money than just make and spend. If you want to build financial stability for you and your family, it's going to take some forethought and a certain amount of risk, just as it did for the first two servants in the parable. As you begin to take control of a few things, you will find it easier to take on more and more responsibility. You may start out struggling just to save ten dollars a week or pay your bills on time, but before you know it, you will have developed the habits and skills that will lead you to bigger and better things: financing a new home or proudly watching your child's college fund grow.

Contrary to what you may think, you can live the so-called good life as a single parent. Make life an adventure for you and your kids, discovering all the non-monetary ways to learn, love, and give from the heart. Always keep in mind the importance of balance in your life, especially where financial issues are concerned. Achieving that balance is totally subjective. Only you know when to stop working and when to start playing with your kids, or socializing with your friends and family. Only you can decide whether a second job is really necessary or how important a retirement or college fund is. You must decide for yourself the exact role money will play in your life.

Checkpoint

- Have you assessed your tangible wealth by completing the financial and spending habits worksheets?
- Have you assessed your intangible wealth by completing the balance sheet?
- Have you allocated your at-risk income to nonessential expenses?
- Have you made the goal-setting process a family affair?
- Are you keeping a written journal to track daily savings?
- Have you thought about ways to produce extra income?
- Are you committed to allocating half of your savings to long-term investments?
- Do your investment choices complement your long-term goals?
- Do you feel more in control of your finances?
- Does your new financial picture reflect a balance between your monetary goals and your personal values?

If you can answer yes to all these questions, go on to chapter 6.

6

Taking Care of You

I stepped from Plank to Plank
A slow and cautious way
The Stars about my Head I felt
About my Feet the Sea.

I knew not but the next
Would be my final inch—
This gave me that precarious Gait
Some call Experience.

—Emily Dickinson

Growing Up with Children

One look at Michelle's picture-perfect family of four, and no one would be the wiser about how she really began her journey into motherhood. Blessed with two active school-aged girls and a husband who adores her, Michelle, at twenty-four, appears to have it all. But it wasn't always the case. She utters a daily prayer of thanks for a life she'll never again take for granted.

Eight years ago, Michelle was catapulted into adulthood like many teenage girls who become pregnant and are forced to make premature choices about their futures. A "carefree teen," as she describes herself, Michelle's idea of having fun was playing in the school band and attending school dances. But then it seemed everything changed overnight, and simplicity was replaced with complex questions. She could no longer identify with the childish problems her friends were facing. She was about to become a mother—a child carrying a child.

Michelle's story is not unlike that of thousands of teens who are faced with raising a child before they themselves have a chance to grow up. It begins with the common misconception that pregnancy only happens to other girls.

"It wasn't something my friends or I ever thought would happen," Michelle recalls. "When I became pregnant, not only did it wake me up, but it was also a wake-up call to a lot of my classmates."

Michelle's decision to raise her baby alone was not an easy one, but she was fortunate to have her parents' support. Michelle also says her strict Catholic upbringing in eastern Ohio was a blessing because it armed her with the faith she needed to make it through the rough times.

"I spent all of my elementary and high school years in Catholic schools, and when I became pregnant during my junior year in high school, I was afraid. But I talked to my principal and he made me feel so comfortable. He gave me a lot of support that really helped me feel better about starting school the following year. Actually, my principal, who was a Catholic priest, discouraged marriage at the time. Every one of my teachers were supportive and helped me out that year. Without them, I may have thought of dropping out of school. But deep down, I knew I was a good student and had a good head on my shoulders."

Michelle says that her initial fears about single parenthood were related to financial and career issues. "I wondered how I was going to support myself and my child. I knew I wanted to go to college someday. Also, having a child at such a young age meant I may never be able to have a good relationship with a man. I wasn't going to be able to date like I had before."

Two years later, Michelle experienced a teen mom's worst nightmare—she got pregnant again.

"I was involved in a very bad, abusive relationship. I didn't know how to get out of it without being physically threatened or hurt. I was feeling trapped and unable to focus on myself. I think if the relationship would have been different, maybe the second pregnancy wouldn't have happened."

Despite the odds against her, and with her family's strong support, Michelle overcame the abusiveness and forged ahead toward her dream of getting a college education.

"My family encouraged me so much," Michelle remembers fondly. "They knew I could do it. If it wasn't for my mom, I would have never been able to make it. She watched both of my children while I attended school at the local technical college. Sometimes, when I would have a long day of classes, she would bring the girls out to school for lunch. She really encouraged me."

Michelle lost her mother to cancer two years ago, which was an emotional downfall for her. Michelle felt completely alone. "My mother was a wonderful person. When she died, I lost not only the person who raised and cared for me, but I also lost the person who helped me raise my own children. I always considered her my kids' father, in a sense, because she and I shared so much of the daily tasks. She took them to the park, the zoo, shopping. She took care of them when I was sick."

Although it was a long road, Michelle completed her two-year degree in civil engineering as a single parent. She glows with pride in recounting those tough years. "Occasionally, I had to cut down my school hours to part-time when I couldn't get the classes I needed. That was frustrating because it was taking more than three years to get a two-year degree. But I always tried to use that down time to spend additional time with my kids.

"I am proud of the decision I made to have both of my children. I am proud to say I have a degree. It was not easy juggling motherhood and school, trying to keep my grades up, but I never wanted to have to depend on someone to support me. I wanted to be educated in a field where I could support myself and my family without the help of someone else. I wanted to be somebody, not fall into the category of so many other young mothers who had to depend on welfare to make it."

Michelle is now married and says she wouldn't trade her present life—or the events leading up to it—for anything. "Yes, I had two children at a very young age. I might not have been able to do all the things my friends were doing, but I have no regrets. All of my experiences, the hardships I've had to overcome, and parenting have made a difference in my life. I am thankful I was able to build a trusting, loving relationship with the wonderful man I married a year ago. He has helped me to understand that not all bad things come from tough circumstances."

According to Michelle, teen moms have the toughest time remembering that they are important. "If you don't like yourself, you will never be able to make the most of your life or your baby's life. More important," she says, "you won't be able to let anyone else in to know you or like you."

❀❀❀❀❀❀❀❀❀❀

"I've forgotten what it's like to be me," one mother said about her three years of single-parent chaos. "We're existing as a family, but I don't exist as an individual. I spend all my time trying to keep up. There's no time for me." One can sympathize with her sentiments, but it is more difficult to accept her rationale. Can situations and circumstances rob us of our individuality or prevent us from experiencing personal growth? Not without our permission. But we can get so caught up in the responsibility of raising children and making ends meet that we forget to partake in a periodic dose of self-indulgence.

Now that you've had some time to think about your goals for the future and work through practical decisions about career and finances, it's time to focus on developing a regular schedule of self-nurturing. It may seem like you've turned your entire life inside out by now, and your self-confidence may be soaring, but be careful. Despite the progress you've made, your fragile sense of self needs to be reinforced, and maybe even reconstructed, in order to go on to tougher, and critically important, parenting tasks. So let's take a temporary detour from problem solving to get acquainted with what feeds our bodies and souls.

This chapter is designed to help you see the significance of guarding your most valuable asset—you. Self-nurturing involves the physical, social, and spiritual aspects of life. The remainder of this chapter will provide easy steps and suggestions for feeding and nurturing these vital areas.

The Importance of Balance

Life is like a wheel, made up of several spokes representing our critical areas of focus. As long as all the spokes are of equal length and weight, the wheel will function smoothly and efficiently. Can you imagine the result if two or three of

the spokes were half the length of the others? The wheel would be lopsided and weak, probably unable to function as it was intended.

Now consider the purpose for which *you* were intended. Think about it. When you are suffering in any one of these areas, things just don't seem to run smoothly. Every one of us has had times when we have suffered physical pain or strain in a relationship. Doesn't it make everything else seem more stressful?

One of the keys to liking and enjoying who you are lies in recognizing your absolute need for balance, especially when you are faced with multiple responsibilities (as most single parents are). Obviously, it is impossible to keep a perfect pace in all areas of life, but it is a good idea to be aware that overemphasis in one area will ultimately cause a shortage in another.

Remembering Childlike Freedom

There's no question: kids seem to have a better sense of natural balance than most adults. Think back to your childhood. Can you remember what the simplest pleasures were? Think hard, because some of them may be events you haven't thought about in years. What about splashing barefoot in mud puddles after a summer storm? What about lying on your back and making angels in the snow or imagining pictures in the clouds? How about blowing bubbles through a ring or puffing away the fuzzy remains of a dandelion? And don't forget the wind in your hair as you raced down a hill on your bike, or the sound of a cracking baseball bat at the Little League game. My favorite childhood memory is the short summer season when fireflies (or lightening bugs, as we called them) lit up the nights. We'd catch as many as we could put in a jar and sit them by our beds to glow in the dark. A symphony of crickets outside the window and a fan blowing the hot humid air around my room lulled me to sleep each night. If I really concentrate, I can almost reproduce the sounds and the smells as if I were there.

It's no wonder children are the least likely to suffer stress-induced illnesses. They see the world in different ways than adults do. For them, it's a world full of wonder, mystery, exploration, interaction with nature, and simplistic ideals. What happens when you give a three-year-old an expensive toy? He or she usually enjoys the box it came in more than anything. Why? Because children that age don't see any difference between the two. Both look interesting and both serve to amuse. The box, however, is simpler. It can be crushed, pounded, written upon, and thrown across the room—all without a single scolding! Children prefer the freedom to act on impulse.

When asked to conjure up special memories of long ago, seldom do we mention the challenge of acing a math test or doing our Saturday chores. Special memories that really capture the essence of childhood are those that feed our senses, remind us of a carefree spirit, or relate to the mysteries of nature. Playing with friends, fishing with Grandpa, or kicking a tin can around in the street—whatever made up your childhood existence constitutes the memories you hold dear in your heart for the rest of your life.

Too often we think adulthood is no place for the trivialities of childhood, and we usually dismiss our youthful memories as belonging to the good old days. But in reality, the responsibilities and rigorous stresses of our adult lives require that we take time for simple childlike freedoms. If we're going to be effective parents and maintain a healthy sense of self, relearning to view the world through a child's eyes is definitely a good place to start.

The Case for Self-Nurturing

Taking time for yourself is like saving money. If you don't allocate it, you probably won't do it. Therefore, the first step in achieving self-acceptance is to set aside a period of time each day, week, and month to feed your spiritual, physical, and social needs. Mark it in your calendar or appointment book. Your first priority in life should be to take care of yourself. You know how flight attendants always ask you to secure your own mask first before assisting a child? The same goes for everyday life.

Barbara, an attorney and mother of twin boys, became a single parent after her husband died in an automobile accident. Like many women in her position, she threw herself into her work and into her sons' hectic sports schedules to avoid the pain. The numbing effect the situation had on her kept her from any desire to socialize with friends, eat balanced meals, or even spend much-needed time relaxing. Consequently, after a year of an out-of-balance lifestyle, Barbara ended up in the hospital from sheer exhaustion. She felt depressed, unloved, and angry. Her doctor's orders: take a long vacation.

What Barbara had failed to do was set aside part of her day to feed and nurture herself, which resulted in her inability to nurture her sons and maintain a career she loved. Understandably, Barbara's grief got in the way of good judgment. In order to practice preventative maintenance in the future, Barbara should block time for herself as if she were her own best client.

Step #1
Make a commitment to self-nurturing.

- Make sure your wheel is in balance and critical areas of focus are in check.
- Start looking at the world through a child's eyes.
- Make daily, weekly, and monthly appointments with yourself.

Effective Stress Reducers

One of the things in life that will induce a low self-esteem and is sure to make you feel old is stress. It comes in a variety of forms, and often creeps up on us without warning, but once we've fallen victim to it, it can be tough to overcome. The following are three areas in which you can take a pro-active approach to avoiding a stressful life.

Diet

All of us know (and many painfully so) that our food intake affects the way we feel and look. If we overeat, we can feel tired and gain weight, which can cause serious health risks and damage self-esteem. If we undereat, or just simply fail to eat the right foods, we can suffer similar health risks, as well as feel less energetic and lack self-confidence. With so much at stake, then, it is vital to pay attention to your body's metabolism and keep your weight within a healthy range. It is also important to eat foods that will provide energy and good nutrition every day.

The busy life of a single parent is not typically conducive to healthy eating patterns. Being prepared is half the battle, however. Here are a few suggestions to help you stay on track:

- Once a week (maybe every Sunday evening), prepare carrots and celery sticks, cut up broccoli and cauliflower, cube a block of cheese, or organize raisins, granola, and wheat crackers. Divide them evenly into five plastic snack bags. Put the bags into your refrigerator's crisper section and pull one out every day to take to work. Add an apple, banana, orange, or any other fruits you like. Rather than eat chips or candy from the vending machine at work, eat from your snack bag.
- Just as preparation is important to your budget, it is also important to eating the right foods. Choose recipes ahead of time that are strong in the four food groups. Some healthy foods can also be expensive. Don't trade off for less-expensive and less-healthy canned or frozen imitations. Instead, buy a small amount and add to salad, pasta, casseroles, or soup. This way, you add other ingredients that are filling, but your family can still eat healthy foods without breaking your budget.
- Healthy eating doesn't have to be time-consuming. Save the big Sunday dinner for Sunday. Plan one big family meal for one weekend night and

make meals during the week that are quick but healthy. A meal of quartered peanut butter sandwiches garnished with carrot sticks, pineapple slices, and cottage cheese is both quick and nutritious. Be creative, and concentrate on eating healthy with everyone around the table together, rather than pressuring yourself to fix traditional meals like your mother used to make.

- Take advantage of slow-cooking recipes you can start in the morning and come home to after work. Many cookbooks contain great recipes for healthy one-pot meals that take a minimal amount of time to prepare.
- Double the recipe of a meal you prepare on the weekend and freeze the leftovers. Casseroles or other freezer-friendly dishes make tasty and nutritious warm-ups for weeknight meals.

Deciding what foods to include in your daily regimen can be a confusing task, given people's inherent need for tradition coupled with conflicting studies about the health dangers and benefits from certain foods. For example, eliminating high-cholesterol foods like meat and dairy products from your diet will not be detrimental to your health as long as you eat a variety of other healthy foods. On the other hand, it cannot be proven that a balanced diet including meat and dairy products will shorten your life, either. It is true that meat and dairy products are among the most expensive food sources, so you may want to keep weekly grocery costs down by avoiding them in the first place, and replacing them with more fruits and vegetables. Whatever you decide, one thing is certain: eating healthy will help you look good, feel positive, and give your family the best chance for a healthy, happy lifestyle.

If you're not convinced that food intake has no effect on you other than weight gain or loss, try the following test:

1. Don't change your eating habits at all for two weeks. Keep a diary, however, of what you eat throughout the day. At the end of each day, jot down your general mood and levels of energy and productivity.
2. Try two weeks of healthy eating, continuing to keep a daily diary of food intake, moods, and energy and productivity levels.
3. At the end of one month, you should have a good record of food intake and how it affected you on a daily basis. Now you can decide how important nutrition is in your daily life. Add these benefits to obvious weight

control and health-risk reductions, and you really have no argument against making a positive change in your eating habits.

Dr. Neil Barnard, in his book *Food for Life,* says:

Our families eat with us. We share similar tastes, and we share all the family times when food plays a central role. As you redesign your menu, it helps to involve your family and friends, for two reasons. First, you need their support. Starting new habits is much easier with their help, and more difficult if they give you a hard time. Second, they need your help in changing their diets, too. If you don't help them improve their diets, you may wish you had.[1]

Do it for them—do it for you!

Exercise

Yuk! Exercise is even worse than dieting. It hurts, it takes time, and it's lonely, especially if we have to do it at 5:00 A.M.! So why bother? Because in addition to being on a well-balanced diet, exercise is the key to a healthy heart, limber muscles (relieving stress), increased energy, and a natural glow—all things single parents need to feel good. Fortunately, deciding to take part in a regular exercise program does not mean you have to join an expensive health club, buy a Nordic Track, or block two hours of your time each day to get it done. Consistency and opportunity are the keys.

Of course, what you decide to do every day depends on your interests, abilities, and schedule. If you're a night owl, morning exercise is probably a noble goal, but unrealistic. Don't set yourself up for failure. You know what you're most likely to stick with. From there, it's a matter of commitment and developing a habit.

Take a brisk twenty-minute walk every day after work with your kids. They can ride their bikes along side you while you try to keep up, or if you have a dog, go for a family and pet outing. Walks can be a great time to talk to your kids about school, their friends, or just shoot the breeze. It's also amazing how a change of scenery and some fresh air can get your mind off the troubles of the day. If weather doesn't permit a good brisk walk, do an indoor workout consisting of a combination of simple exercises like running in place (or around the house), jumping jacks, toe touches, sit-ups, leg stretches, and so forth. If you get the kids involved, they'll have fun and will be sure to not let you forget exercise time. It may seem like the last thing you want to do after a long day at work, but after work is precisely the best time to exercise because it will wind you down instantly and help you get a better night's rest.

Here are a few tips to help you keep up the pace:

- Lay out your workout clothes and shoes every night before you go to bed, so when you get home from work the next day, you'll be ready to make the transition.
- It's better to exercise on an empty stomach. Start dinner before exercise time and work out while it is simmering or in the oven.
- Make a chart of exercises to do during each workout and have your kids count for you and mark each one off as they're completed.
- Alternate between aerobic and muscle-strengthening exercises. Take walks on Monday, Wednesday, and Friday, and work muscles (sit-ups, leg lifts, weight lifting) on Tuesday, Thursday, and Saturday. You might rest on Sunday, or save the weekend days for fun exercise with friends, like tennis or swimming. Do something for twenty or more minutes every day.
- Reward everyone for sticking with it. Give yourself a star every day you exercise and trade the stars in for an occasional treat, like shopping or going to a movie.
- Commit to daily exercise for two weeks (no cheating). Then ask yourself if you feel stronger, more energetic, less tired, and more confident. Chances are, the answer will be yes.

Relationships

Most people tend to feel good about themselves when they're surrounded by a network of people who care for them and want to see them succeed. Your current stress may be multiplied by relationships you have with people who do not fit into this category. One of the toughest things to do in life is end a destructive relationship, especially one that has withstood a long period of time. Many times, we don't even realize a relationship is bad for us until we get into trouble or are deeply hurt by it. The best guard against this is to consciously seek out positive relationships. There's no better way to discover, and feel motivated to eradicate, a bad relationship than experiencing a good one. The comparison is usually shocking. Analyze the kinds of people you are spending time with and ask yourself whether these relationships are helping you to grow and become healthier, or tearing you down emotionally and physically.

I believe all single parents would benefit from developing a "survival network" as soon as possible—that is, a group of people who will be there to see you through all the many trials single parents invariably face over the years. Some of the people in your network will be close friends; others will be acquaintances whom you will need for specific services in the event of a problem. Your network might look something like this:

Personal Survival Network

- Personal friends: male and female single parents, married couples, older mentors
- Relatives: parents, grandparents, sisters and brothers, aunts and uncles
- Professional counselors: counselor, pastor, minister, rabbi, priest
- Health providers: family physician, dentist, gynecologist, eye doctor, pharmacist, veterinarian
- Automobile advisors: auto insurance agent, mechanic, auto club representative
- Household advisors: home insurance agent, heating and cooling repair persons, plumber, general repair people
- Financial/Legal advisors: local bank representative, attorney, financial consultant
- General confidants: daycare providers, coworker(s), post office worker, grocery store manager

---

To assist you in compiling your survival network, complete Worksheet E in the Appendix. You don't have to do this all at once. Write down the obvious people first, but then commit to finding one or more network members every week. All it takes is a phone call or a personal visit. Avoid sending letters or just leaving messages, because the whole idea behind this is to become personally acquainted with the people on your list. Your goal is not only to establish ties with people who will come to your aid when you are in need, but also to develop friendships with people who will take an interest in your ongoing success.

Once you've established your network, keep in touch with the members regularly to let them know how you're doing. You may be able to offer your services in exchange for others' or simply to show your appreciation for their help. For example, baby-sit for a friend, cook dinner for someone who is ill, or call a member just to check in. For those on your list whom you will probably only call when there's a problem (mechanic, repair person, attorney), be fair when they help you out. Some people may understand that your budget is tight and may not want to take money for their services. That's great, but you can still show your appreciation by doing something special like making cookies for them or sending a card with a small payment (whatever you can afford). That shows them you're not trying to use them, but rather, trying to maintain a positive relationship.

Where do you find these people? Believe it or not, trustworthy people do still roam the earth, but you have to be willing to spend time searching them out. Churches and synagogues are the best place to find people who will genuinely care about you, although just because someone affiliates him- or herself with a religious group does not a good person make.

Get involved in community clubs or with groups of people whose interests are similar to yours (Parents Without Partners, divorce or widow recovery groups, PTA, charitable organizations, garden clubs, and so on). You can also get referrals from these people.

Parents, married and single, often find companionship with each other by attending their children's extracurricular activities. You might develop good relationships with people you meet at your child's karate class, baseball game, swim meet, piano recital, or daycare function. A common interest between children might be enough for you to bond with other parents.

Coworkers are also a good resource because you already have at least one thing in common and because you spend so much time on the job. Be careful to observe company rules about spending personal time with another coworker, however, especially on company time.

Bars, nightclubs, parties, and the like are the last places to look for long-lasting relationships—mostly because of the presence of alcohol, which tends to impair good judgment. There's nothing wrong with going out for a good time now and then, but don't rely on the nightclub circuit as your source for meeting people. Besides, your chances of finding the kind of people who will care about you are pretty low. The other suggestions mentioned here are much less risky and will probably offer plenty of possibilities.

Step #2
Avoid stress: Eat right, exercise, and build positive relationships.

- Consciously link food intake with how it will make you feel.
- Set aside twenty minutes each day for regular exercise.
- Develop a personal survival network.

Get in Touch with Your Inner Self

When you're at home, the kids are visiting your ex, your friends are busy, and sleep won't come, you are most vulnerable to feelings of loneliness. If you don't like who you are or who you've become, you will have an extremely difficult time being alone without feeling lonely. It will simply be too painful to spend time thinking about the present, reflecting on the past, or planning for the future. Loneliness is especially likely if you're around people who don't really understand you or your beliefs, in part because you don't know how to express them.

Getting to know your inner self, or spiritual side, is one of the most enriching experiences a human being will ever encounter. Unfortunately, this understanding doesn't just descend from the heavens one day in a bolt of lightening or a booming voice. Most often, it's a slow and subtle process. Less often, such as during a life-changing event, it can unfold quickly. But even in those cases, time is needed to fully understand the shift. However it happens, learning about your innermost self is something that takes time, endurance, and patience.

Shortly after my divorce, I felt a strong need to begin writing. I had so many wild emotions going through my head. I thought I had figured out so much of life, until I was faced with a family crisis. In one fell swoop, it seemed I knew nothing. To sort out my feelings, I began a nightly journal, consisting mostly of prayers and commentary on a variety of emotions and subjects. It was not only extremely therapeutic, but it allowed me to develop a much-needed personal value system—something I had lacked prior to this time. I had always gleaned my beliefs from someone else: spouse, family members, friends, church leaders. For the first time in my life, I was faced with discerning a system of beliefs based on my inner voice. It was grueling, and it was gratifying. It was also the discovery process that would truly change my life—not the effects of divorce, poverty, or single parenthood, as I had originally thought. I can't recommend a specific method for discovering your inner self, because it is the most personal journey anyone can take. I can, however, describe the process and emphasize the importance of taking a spiritual path of some kind.

The biggest barrier you will encounter along the way is the urge to close up. The emotions leading up to single parenthood are often in response to the loss or destruction of a significant relationship. Feelings of mistrust usually follow—whether it's mistrust in other people or in God. Then, somehow, this mistrust is imposed inward. This distrust can rob its victim of peace, happiness, and contentment. It becomes a self-fulfilling circle: when we feel defeated, we tend to lack self-confidence, and when we lack self-confidence, we tend to fail.

There are many roads through the process of self-examination. Sometimes it helps to attend a religious service or function. Other times, the process may be prompted by reading insightful books and talking to friends and family members who care. You may even start your journey like I did through daily prayer and journal keeping. The first step is to be open to the experience. Second, you must be willing to search for the path you are most comfortable with. I've seen many people "find themselves" through religion, only to find in the end that they have lost themselves in a strict system that dictates beliefs rather than promotes soul searching. This is not the kind of path that will lead to a healthy self-esteem or value system. Read a lot of material, talk with scores of people, and attend lectures, functions, and mind-expanding programs *before* you make any decisions about where your spiritual journey will head.

Third, don't let anyone pressure you. This is not something that has to be decided quickly. Allow yourself the time and space to figure it all out. Don't pressure yourself, and by all means, give yourself room to fall, room to learn. Most religions preach forgiveness and redemption. If you really want to experience the benefits of knowing yourself in a spiritual way and use this knowledge to become a better person,

- learn to forgive others
- learn to forgive yourself
- take what you've learned and develop a system of values
- live in accordance with your values
- guide your children in these values

Step #3
Discover what's inside.

- Be open to self-examination.
- Seek out people and information to help you make wise decisions.
- Be patient and allow yourself time to learn.
- Develop and live by your personal value system.

Choosing Healthy Dating Relationships

A funny thing happens when you begin to really like yourself: others begin to like you, too. Sooner or later, you will confront choices that involve intimate relationships. There's no doubt that getting attention and feeling wanted in a dating relationship will improve your self-esteem. Everyone wants and needs to feel approval, especially when it involves romantic feelings. But there are dangers here that warrant discussion before you go searching for Prince Charming or Cinderella to validate your existence.

Romantic relationships are magnetic in nature. It takes more than good looks or charm to attract one person to another. Personality traits, family backgrounds, belief systems, economic classes, social skills—a vast array of magnetic particles cause sparks to fly between two people. Because people tend to attract partners with similar lifestyles and ideals, it's important to first examine yourself to make sure that you will like what you attract.

For instance, some negative relationships are extremely dangerous because one person is passive and the other is controlling. This is the case in many domestic-abuse cases. Why does a woman who has been repeatedly beaten by her husband get a divorce and go on to marry another abuser? Because passive types are so strongly attracted to controller types, and vice versa, that the pattern can only be broken if one or the other recognizes it and changes his or her behavior. By the same token, many relationships are productive because they consist of two positively connected individuals, each with a healthy self-esteem and commitment to the relationship.

How can you tell a good spark from a bad? Usually, you can't at first. The best way to be sure you are on the right track with someone is to spend a great deal of time getting to know your inner self. I became involved in a relationship with someone soon after my divorce. After ten years of marriage and a lot of pain, it was exciting, to say the least, to have someone else pay attention to me—someone who made me feel special and beautiful. I felt "in love" with this person and truly thought I was going to spend the rest of my life with him.

Luckily, we took it slow, and eventually our true colors began to show. I soon discovered that our initial attraction was based on our shared pain. We had both experienced painful breakups with our ex-partners and enjoyed talking to one another about our similar circumstances. We filled a void for each other that our former spouses had once filled. But when the healing began, we realized we had less in common with one another than we originally thought. We gradually grew apart. Had we rushed into a marriage, we would have been headed for a lifetime of struggles.

It is often difficult to separate emotional attachments from those that represent solid, lifelong fulfillment. That is why I can't stress enough the importance of working on your own personal growth first. A relationship should only serve to bring a deeper meaning and higher quality to your life. Don't compromise for anything less. If you start becoming the kind of person you appreciate, love, respect, and admire, you will no doubt begin to attract the types of people who mirror these qualities. Remember, love is a controlled decision, not an emotional infatuation. If your feelings for another person are out of control, you are not yet ready to make a decision about loving that person for life.

Step #4
Embrace dating relationships with caution.

- Make your own personal growth your first priority.
- Become the kind of person you want to attract.
- Remember, love is a controlled decision.

Kids and Dating

If you have determined that you are ready for a healthy dating relationship, there are some important questions associated with dating as a single parent. The most common are as follows:

- When do I introduce my new partner to my children?
- How do I deal with my children's jealousy?
- What if my children don't like my partner?
- How long should we date before deciding on marriage?
- Is counseling recommended before considering a blended family?

These are all important, yet difficult, questions to answer with a blanket statement. How you deal with each specific issue will likely depend on the length of time you've been a single parent, the ages of your children, and the personalities and temperaments of everyone involved.

Introductions

When to introduce the children to your new dating partner has a common sense answer that is too often ignored. Children who have experienced the death of one parent, or who have experienced divorce, will be sensitive to losing another significant person in their lives. Don't be surprised if they keep their distance for a long time after you've made the initial introduction. This is a natural defense against getting hurt by another loss. Be extremely sensitive to these defenses.

It's easy to want to spend every waking hour with someone when you feel head over heels in love, but keep a clear head. Create some distance between you and your new partner by blocking time to spend alone with your kids. This will give you a chance to take a step back and examine the new relationship. It will also help your kids feel more secure about the changes taking place. Last, but not least, it can provide a clue as to how your partner will react to your putting a priority on your parenting responsibilities.

A good rule of thumb is to keep your dating life separate from your family life at least until after you have had a chance to test the relationship for yourself. When both you and your partner feel comfortable that the relationship has a long-term future, make the introductions, but don't expect your children and your new friend to begin doing a number of activities together. Let the relationships unfold naturally. If you and your new partner truly want to foster a successful transition, your example of patience and respect toward one another in a horizontal relationship should set the tone for the vertical relationships you expect between step=parents and children.

Take things slowly and keep the relationship in front of the children at arm's length. Overnight stays while the children are around are simply not a good idea. It will only cause more tension for everyone involved and will appear to the children that you are trying to force a "new family" concept on them. Save kissing and touching for when the children are not around. This will help them get to know your partner without feeling embarrassed when you're all together. Imagine sitting around watching your mother and a strange man necking on the couch (yuk)!

Jealousy

Children are prone to jealousy toward your new relationship, particularly when they feel the threat of losing you to another person. Having already lost one parent, children can have difficulty with the thought of losing you, as well. When they become overly protective, express disapproval of your new dating life, or misbehave to get attention, do not retaliate with anger. But do not stop dating to appease them, either. Rather, listen to what they have to say. Continually assure them that you will not make a permanent decision about bringing someone new into all of your lives unless you feel it will be good for everyone. Ask them to trust you and be especially loving toward them during this time.

How Long Is Long Enough?

Some experts say you should wait at least a year before marrying someone to give you an opportunity to experience the four seasons together. Others say most couples know early on whether or not the chemistry is going to be right, so time is insignificant. Actually, time is not the most important factor; what is important is taking the right amount of time to make a good decision. Shared value systems and a commitment to a loving, long-term relationship are what two people really need to decide whether or not their marriage will be successful. Exploring each others' value systems will take time, so whatever it takes, take it.

My new husband and I spent a couple of months talking about such important issues as religious beliefs, raising children, personal freedom, political views, the importance of independence and teamwork, and so forth. We started a journal, writing letters back and forth to one another about our feelings in these areas. When you have to put it in writing, it adds a level of commitment to your thoughts (something that can be a little frightening, but definitely enriching). After spending ten years in a mismatched marriage that ended in divorce, I was not willing to jump into it again without a great deal of forethought. Although I'm sure we were both influenced by our strong emotional feelings toward one another at the time, it was a good idea to get our opinions out in the open. Knowing we shared beliefs about important issues, and shared respect for one another and a commitment to the relationship, it was easy to say "I do" when the time came.

When you begin to talk more seriously with your partner about marriage, then it is appropriate to take the relationship between your partner and your children to a new level of closeness. At that point, you might want to have a sit-down discussion with everyone to talk about the possibilities of blending the family and spending more time together. Allow your kids to express their feelings about the relationship, and encourage them to be patient with your partner, just as your partner should be willing to be patient with them. Remember, you were a parent before you were this person's date. Finding out how well your partner accepts the package deal is very important to your decision to bond your life with him or her. Observing interactions while gradually spending more time together is always a good idea. Expect awkwardness, allow for strong feelings, and don't rush the future. Relax.

Teddi Sanford and Mickie Padorr Silverstein, in their book *Marrying Again,* give these basic guidelines to help single parents deal with marriage:

Before you decide you are ready to remarry, come to terms with what you owe your children and what you owe yourself. You owe your children a harmonious environment in which they are loved and accepted, not just tolerated. You owe them a step-parent who should not try to become a substitute for the other parent, but who should feel respected by your children—not treated like an intruder. What you don't owe your children is the right to own you until they are ready to cut the apron strings and get on with their own lives. You don't owe them your chance for happiness and a new life, even if it means disrupting their lives by moving to another city or home. Children are very resilient, and they adjust.[3]

What about Counseling?

Counseling is always a good idea, but it definitely cannot hurt when you're considering a life-changing decision. If your children seem to be warming up to the new relationship, and you and your partner feel completely comfortable with each other's values and commitments, however, counseling is probably not necessary, unless problems arise later.

If, on the other hand, your children are expressing disapproval or jealousy, and especially if you and your partner are having difficulty agreeing on important issues, by all means, seek counseling. It's important to find out early if you or your partner needs to make significant personal changes before entering into a marital relationship together. Oftentimes, couples who are contemplating remarriage may find there are unresolved conflicts from a previous relationship. If these things are not addressed, they will definitely cause problems in the new marriage. Make the intelligent decision to enter marriage with a healthy heart.

**Step #5
Approach marriage cautiously, with
sensitivity and practicality.**

- Understand your children's natural defenses.
- Gradually allow a bond to develop between your kids and your new
  partner.
- Confirm shared value systems and long-term commitment.
- Seek counseling, if necessary, to assist in the transition.

In a Nutshell

Liking myself had a lot to do with feeling confident and proud in my role as a
single parent. Eating right, exercising, thinking more like a child, and acting like
a responsible adult were all important factors in building my self-esteem.
Ultimately, however, I knew I had reached the point of self-acceptance when I
began feeling joy in my everyday existence. Here is an excerpt from my journal
back in 1992:

*Other than the occasional hum of the refrigerator and the sweet sound
of one of my children's snores, the entire house seems completely undisturbed
and frozen in time. If it were not for the steady ticking of the living room
clock, I would be convinced of it. For the time that I choose to remain in this
somewhat thoughtless state, it doesn't seem to matter what is going on in the
world outside of my humble abode. Murderous acts are being committed
across town and families are weeping and wailing in the midst of a crisis,
but for me and mine, this is our world—at least for tonight. I say a heart-
felt prayer of thanks for another day of health and life, and as I glance
around this glorious room that I have dressed in a decor selected only for me,
I notice each detail—each piece of furniture and accessory that has a history all of its own. I do not live in a mansion. I am far from what some may
consider the upper class. But I sit here and savor with all my senses the wonderful feeling of being home. A place of safety. A haven of rest at the end of
a challenging day. Yes, tomorrow morning at 7:00 A.M. sharp, the chattering*

of children tormenting one another and the clanging of cereal bowls will remind me that another day is beginning and anything could happen. For now, though, I find pleasure and sweet serenity in knowing that I have once again accomplished another day.

Just as happiness is not in obtaining everything you want, but in wanting everything you have, joy comes from recognizing that the quality of life is only increased when you are able to embrace it with peace. Taking care of you involves bringing into balance the critical areas of life we have discussed in this chapter. Commit today, for you and your family, to strike a balance. Find balance. Find peace. Find joy.

Checkpoint

- Have you made a commitment to self-nurturing?
- Are you paying more attention to eating habits?
- Are you committed to a regular exercise plan?
- Do you have a survival network in place?
- Are you working on developing your spirituality and personal value system?
- Is your personal growth a priority over dating relationships?
- Are you sensitive to your children's natural defenses against another loss?
- Do you recognize the importance of your happiness and the chance for a new life?

If you can answer yes to all these questions, go on to chapter 7.

PART THREE:

Child Development

7

GUIDING YOUR CHILD WITH EFFECTIVE DISCIPLINE

If you bungle raising your children, I don't think whatever else you do well matters very much.　　　　　　　—Jacqueline Kennedy Onassis

Surviving and Thriving

Chris and his three children, Richard, sixteen, Timothy, fourteen, and Elizabeth, eleven, spend as much time together at home in Worcester, England, as their busy schedules permit. They enjoy swimming, bowling, hiking, playing badminton—it's all part of what this family does to solidify their bond and heal their souls. Two years ago, they lost a wife and mother, not through a bitter divorce, addiction, or neglect. Against her will and theirs, cancer claimed Sandie's life, leaving Chris and their children to put the pieces back together on their own.

Following his wife's death, Chris quickly assumed the dual role of mother and father. There was no one to blame, no one to take half of the responsibility, no one to relieve him when things got tough. Losing a second income meant only one paycheck; there were no child support payments to claim. But he was determined to make it work. Chris knew that facing the arduous task of parenting alone, while he and his adolescent children were grieving, was going to be a difficult road.

"For the widowed parent, raising children can be tricky. I had to always take my frame of mind into account. I remember being very sensitive just after losing Sandie. I was prone to overreacting to minor infractions that I would have normally ignored."

Chris has been able to help his children adjust by encouraging them to express themselves and by making their wants and needs a priority. "For the most part, my life now is focused on my children. It is their accomplishments that bring me the most joy. Recently my son completed a model airplane that we intended to take out and fly on the following Saturday. However, while driving home on Friday, I realized that my schedule would be pressing on that day. I was concerned I might not be able to devote the time he would want at the flying field, especially if the model flew well and he wanted to prolong our flying session. So I revised the schedule by postponing the tasks I had planned for Friday evening and decided to take him out flying instead. I sprung the surprise as soon as I reached home. While I changed out of my business suit, he prepared the model and flight box. This meant a complete change of plans for the evening, but it gave me the free slot I needed on Saturday and it let him know that I was looking after his interests, that I wanted to share his enjoyment."

Chris says single parenting has been a challenge, but it's all a matter of good planning. "My circumstances and the busy pace of life limit the quality time I can devote to their needs, so I am keenly aware of the need to use that time to its greatest effect. This results in a busy, intense schedule. So we fit things in when there is a vacant slot in my diary."

Chris's children, despite the closeness they've developed since their mother's death, are not immune to the many challenges facing all kids their age. According to Chris, however, setting proper boundaries at home is the key to their success. "Treat them like infants and they behave like infants. Treat them like mature individuals and they will rise to one's expectations. They have to share the load with me. I can't do everything that Sandie and I would have otherwise shared. So they have responsibilities in the home, and they are expected to carry these out. If they fail to do so, it's not a case of 'having done wrong,' but rather 'having let me down.'

"The basic household activities are run to a weekly schedule, and I have a set routine which allows me to keep these chores under control. To accomplish this, I need their cooperation. As an example, I insist that my children care for their own rooms. This involves them ensuring that their dirty laundry is in the basket before the times I wash the laundry, which is on Saturday and early Tuesday morning. If they fail to do so, then the machine is loaded without their dirty laundry. I will not go to their rooms and collect it.

"Of course, the 'knock on' effect is that there is twice as much laundry for the next session, resulting in additional time being required to press the clean clothes. However, the extra time is taken from their schedules. I may transfer certain tasks from my schedule to theirs to compensate for the extra time I have to spend on their laundry, or I will cancel a planned leisure activity. This way, they understand that the problem is of their own making. They feel the result of their failure to comply with our domestic schedule. It teaches them that their actions have had an effect on the whole family."

Chris says he and his children have been through a lot together, but he is still the parent—the one they look to for help and guidance. He says he gladly accepts the responsibilities that come with parenting alone.

"Sandie's death taught me how precious life is. Soon, my kids will be out of the house and on their own. I've got to make the most of being a parent right now."

❀❀❀❀❀❀❀❀❀❀

The greatest misconception parents can have is believing their children are unaware of what is going on around them. Disregarding how children interpret actions, words, and feelings could be the most serious mistake a parent will ever make. In this chapter you will learn how your love and example are elements of a vital parenting foundation—a foundation on which every successful discipline plan is built.

Chapter 6 gave you some ideas for self-examination. With this as your base, you are better prepared to begin guiding your children through effective discipline. Obviously, everything written about effective parenting today cannot be presented here. Rather, this information should serve as a guide, to help you learn the fundamentals of a good discipline system, and to implement and enforce a plan that works for you.

First and foremost, there is no best way to discipline, because so much of it depends on your family's lifestyle, background, culture, personalities, and goals. However, there are some fundamental concepts. These are illustrated in the parenting pyramid on page 131 and form the foundation of any effective discipline plan. Starting at the bottom of the pyramid, we will work our way to the top, with each level building on the next. As one level of action is completed, the next level of values resulting from the action will be discussed.

What's in a Word?

Merriam-Webster defines *discipline* as "training that corrects, molds or perfects." I think all agree that none of us is trying to perfect our children when we exercise discipline, although our kids may see it differently. The key word in this definition is training. Throughout this chapter, I encourage the use of different words when describing discipline, or training, techniques. Believe it or not, the mood of a word can have a great impact on the way we feel about its meaning, and ultimately the way we react when we hear it. Remember the words diet and budgeting in chapter 5? Replacing them with eating plan or spending plan evokes a more positive response. Just as discipline can be replaced with training, we'll also talk about household skills rather than chores, and guidelines instead of rules. This may seem insignificant to you now, but wait and see. Choosing the positive over the negative will ultimately change the way you view your job of parenting, or shall we say role?

The Parenting Pyramid

A single mother wrote to me, asking a common question: "I want so much for my children. I want to equip them with the skills to make better decisions than I have made. How do I know if I'm really making a difference in my children's lives?" My answer to her was, "You are making a difference, just by virtue of expressing love and concern for their welfare." Unfortunately, a proactive question like hers isn't asked often enough these days. Instead, many parents are asking in retrospect, "How did it get this way? Where did I lose control?"

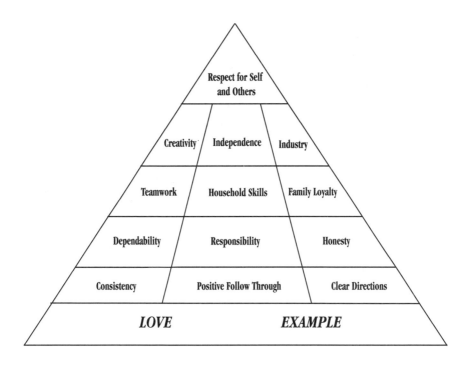

Like I said before, your example is vital to building a strong parenting plan. Example is not enough, however. Love is what will give meaning to the example. It doesn't take a rocket scientist to be a loving parent. But it does take a loving parent to raise a responsible child. For most people, parental love is instinctual. Many will say unequivocally, "Of course I love my children." But only when you combine your deep, heart-felt love for your children with a strong example of character will you have the solid foundation necessary to an effective parenting plan. For many of you, it may be a matter of rediscovering feelings of love for your children, or merely looking at them in a different light.

It's easy to take our children for granted and become a passive parent. It is not so easy to recognize their true value and worth and decide to "make a difference," as the woman wrote to me. It takes hard work, dedication, and commitment— like all good things in life. A foundation of love is the only driver that can keep a parent going, and committed to the goal. Before contemplating the methods of discipline you will implement, or even what the key elements will be, you must commit to love and example as the driving forces of your plan.

Step #1
Love and example constitute the
foundation of good parenting.

- Be aware of how your children interpret your words and actions.
- Don't take children for granted; see them in a different light.
- Guard against regret; decide to take a proactive approach.

The First Three Rules of Effective Training

In his book *Back in Control,* Gregory Bodenhamer outlines three ways parents lose control of their children: inconsistency, unclear directions, and ineffective follow-through. To illustrate, he asks three questions:

1. Are your children likely to be consistent in obeying rules that you aren't consistent in enforcing?
2. If you don't clearly state your rules, whose interpretation of those rules are your children likely to use, yours or theirs?
3. If you don't effectively follow through and enforce your own rules, are your children likely to follow through and enforce them on themselves?[1]

All parents hate to hear that they must be consistent, precise, and true to their threats. Sometimes our busy daily lives just aren't conducive to this kind of enforcement. I remember feeling so tired after a long day at work that I totally tuned my kids out in the evenings. I let them do outrageous things I wouldn't normally tolerate. This didn't happen daily, but it did happen. Occasionally, I lost my drive to be consistent, precise, and reliable, but it didn't make me a bad parent.

Although these three rules are paramount to a solid discipline plan, it is vital for a parent to first accept the fact that he or she cannot realistically play the role of the perfect parent, because kids will never buy it—nor can anyone humanly maintain it. Try to understand and accept your weaknesses, while also recognizing that consistency, clear directions, and good follow-through are the next level of the parenting pyramid's foundation.

Salley Shannon, contributing editor to *Working Mother* magazine, says, "the secret to being a good parent is to focus on what you do best and relax about the rest." Shannon says parents must

- identify what they do best with their children;
- abandon unrealistic expectations; and
- let other significant adults, teachers, and relatives fill the gaps.[2]

If you're naturally a patient person, be proud of your ability to watch Barney with your child twenty times a week. Maybe playfulness or a great sense of humor are your strong points. Whatever your strengths, focus most of your time using them creatively. Work on your weaknesses, but don't let them ruin your confidence. Ask for help from others who may be better in those areas. Once you understand the strengths and weaknesses of your parenting style, you will be better equipped to choose a discipline plan that will be effective. Accepting yourself will also help you to be more accepting of your children's imperfections. Contrary to popular belief, being honest with yourself and letting your kids see that you are not always at your best will not make you weak. In fact, you are more likely to gain their respect by revealing your human side and being committed to doing your best in spite of it.

Step #2
Customize your parenting plan based on your individual strengths and weaknesses.

- Before implementing a plan, ask yourself:
    Is this a plan I can implement consistently?
    Can I communicate it clearly to my kids?
    Can I realistically follow through with the consequences?
- Accept yourself; don't be afraid to show your human side.
- Accentuate the positive; figure out what you do best and do it often!

Guidelines and Consequences

Only a child with boundaries learns to appreciate freedom. Just as laws and regulations govern our adult lives to promote safety, health, and well-being, guidelines are necessary for children to transform them into responsible, law-abiding citizens. As much as children whine and complain about their boundaries, there is no doubt that they function better when they know what is expected of them, and what the consequences are for failing to meet those expectations.

Have you ever started a job with a vague description about what you were supposed to do every day? At first, it's not so bad since you have the freedom to make up the rules as you go. Eventually, however, it catches up with you, and when the boss reprimands you for not doing something you didn't even know you were supposed to be doing, everyone becomes frustrated, oftentimes looking for others to blame. That's essentially what parents do when they treat their kids as if they were born understanding their parents' expectations. So, then, you must communicate your expectations clearly if you want them to be met.

Before making your expectations known, however, examine the motivation behind them. In her book *Your Child's Self-Esteem,* Dorothy Corkille Briggs writes, "each of us sees our children to some degree through a haze of filters born of our past experiences, personal needs, and cultural values. They all combine to form a network of expectations. And these expectations become yardsticks by which we measure a child."[3] Briggs warns not to use borrowed expectations ("That's the way I was raised") or those that fulfill our own childhood dreams ("My kid will be a better baseball player than I was"). Instead, she suggests, our expectations are more likely to be in line if based on facts of child development, our own keen observation of our children, and considering past and present pressures facing them. To help you determine your expectations and how you might construct guidelines and consequences accordingly, take a moment to complete Worksheet F in the Appendix.

It takes as much integrity for a parent to develop guidelines and enforce them as it does for children to follow them. Again, your love and example will be the best training tools. Developing guidelines will be the simplest task, since you should know by now what your expectations are and what kinds of values and life lessons you want your children to learn. Developing consequences will be more difficult, however. Consequences constitute the follow-through. They solidify the entire system. There are three types of consequences: natural, related, and imposed.

If your son leaves his bike out, when he knows he's supposed to lock it in the garage every night, and it gets stolen, he has experienced a natural consequence of life. You can nag him nightly about putting the bike away (naturally trying to protect a monetary investment), but when he wakes up one morning and it is gone, suddenly the value you have been trying to teach him hits home. Natural consequences are the most painful for the parent, because sometimes it is necessary to let children learn the hard way. These are by far the most effective consequences, but are not appropriate for all situations.

When you tell your daughter that you will remove the phone from her room if she violates the thirty-minute limit on phone time per night, and you follow through by removing the phone after she violates that limit, your daughter has suffered a related consequence. Related consequences are most effective when natural consequences aren't practical. The only natural consequence your daughter will suffer as a result of spending too much time on the phone will be an aching ear and possibly a grouchy disposition from too little sleep. Given most teenagers' social priorities, these will probably not be painful enough to make her comply. So in this case, a related consequence works well.

Imposed consequences are aimed at making sure a behavior doesn't occur again. Because they tend to be harsh, they should be used sparingly. Imposed consequences are closest to punishments. Many parents use imposed consequences such as grounding to enforce curfews or respond to other violations, but they can also be used when verbal requests for a behavior change are unsuccessful.

As an example, let's say you are having difficulty getting your kids to pick up after themselves (this is quite a stretch, I'm sure). They leave book bags, gym gear, and hairbrushes lying all over the house. The last thing you want to do is impose a harsh consequence for a minor infraction, but there doesn't seem to be an effective natural or related consequence that fits this situation. Give your kids the benefit of the doubt. Talk to them first (don't threaten). Ask them to please be more careful about picking up their things around the house. Let them know it makes sense to keep their belongings in the right places because it will save time when they are ready to use them, and hope they know you well enough to expect you will take action if they don't respond to firm discussion.

Then, wait and see. More than likely, words won't be enough to change their habits. Give it a week. If you are still tripping over their belongings, put them on notice. Don't be vague about what the guideline will be. Make it clear that every evening at 9:00 or every afternoon at 4:00, or whatever time you expect the house to be in order on a daily basis, you want their belongings put away in the proper places. You might tell them that if you find something out of its place at the end of the day, you will put it in a box where it can only be retrieved with money—maybe $1 per item. By the way, that includes schoolbooks (which will impose a natural consequence when their teachers reprimand them for not having their books in class).

A note of caution: Imposed consequences may be the most painful for children, but they place a heavier burden on parents, who have to enforce them. Remember, the tougher it is to enforce a consequence, the less likely you are to follow through. And because follow-through is vital to success, don't threaten a consequence you can't or won't realistically enforce.

Finally, be flexible and don't be too proud to change the guidelines when things don't appear to be working. Parenting involves a lot of trial and error. We're not maintaining computer equipment here; we're molding and shaping complicated human lives. Virginia Stowe, founder and director of the Parenting Resource Center in New York City, says, "No tactic works 100 percent of the time. So be ready to shift gears and try different approaches. When parents discipline their children with support and respect, they become much more fun to be with."[4]

Level Three:
The Effects of Building the First Two Levels

Parenting starts with a strong foundation of love and example. Making a commitment to consistency, positive follow-through, and communication reinforces this foundation as you set guidelines and consequences for your children. Devoting yourself to these standards in your parenting plan will foster dependability, responsibility, and honesty in your kids. They will learn they can depend on you to follow through with consequences, as they also learn to be dependable in following specific guidelines. They will begin to understand the importance of taking responsibility for their actions, as they make choices based on the guidelines and consequences you've established.

In addition, honesty is encouraged through this discipline strategy by your demonstration of consistency between words and actions. By consistently keeping your word (doing what you say you'll do), you are building trust and promoting an honest relationship with your kids. With these important pieces of the foundation in place, you can now begin to focus on teaching the skills that will foster the next level of values on the parenting pyramid.

Step #3
Set and enforce boundaries.

• Understand your expectations.
• Have a clear idea of what values you want to teach.
• Develop natural, related, and imposed consequences.
• Be flexible; allow room for change and growth.

The Value of an Effective Work System

As old-fashioned as it may sound, a strong work ethic goes a long way toward teaching personal and social responsibility. Not only does practical experience in the home prepare a child for the rigorous workplace, it gives children a proving ground to test complex situations and ideas he or she will inevitably encounter in adulthood. The concepts of teamwork, family loyalty, and household skills are the third level on the parenting pyramid. These ideas are best translated to implementing an effective work/reward system for your children. Keep in mind your children's ages, skill levels, and experience as you consider the ideas and suggestions that follow.

Why do children need to work? Simply because being a team member in a family is important. Serving others is important. Belonging, being needed and valued, is important. Malcolm W. Klein, in his book *The American Street Gang,* talks about one of the reasons our youth are increasingly becoming involved in gangs:

Belonging—having the status of gang membership, the identity with a particular gang, the sense (correct or otherwise) that in the gang there is protection from attack—becomes very important, very rewarding to the member. It provides what he has not obtained from his family, in school, or elsewhere in his community.[5]

Give your children the chance to belong at home, not just because you exist as a family, but because there is something in the family that is worthwhile—something that makes them feel like valuable members. This can be accomplished through a structured and rewarding family work system.

The Importance of Family Meetings

"The family that meets together and plans together is more likely to be a family that works together," says Patricia H. Sprinkle in her book *Do I Have To?*[6] As much as I hesitate to compare family units to business entities, it is clear that any group wanting to achieve teamwork must have an agenda. Clear-cut goals, individual involvement, and appropriate rewards and consequences are all part of the success of most businesses. Running a successful family system involves many of the same ideas, although the players are more intimately connected and emotionally driven.

Holding a family meeting is the best way to begin acclimating your kids to the concept of teamwork. Children as young as three years old can understand the simple workings of a family meeting as long as you choose your words and the subject matter appropriately. The beauty of family meetings is that they can change with your family as your children mature and you gain confidence in your parenting style.

How often should you have family meetings? As often as is comfortable and necessary. Some families like them once a week, others once per month, and some like mine prefer a more flexible schedule. I found that scheduling family meetings too frequently placed a heavy burden on me to organize, perform, and follow through. In going back to our three questions, I could not realistically be consistent, precise, and follow through with weekly or monthly meetings. So I geared the meetings to fit my personality and schedule. We have meetings on January 1 (a good time to make resolutions), at the beginning of the summer, at the beginning of the new school year, or whenever schedules or needs change. These periodic meetings are somewhat longer than they would be if we held them more frequently, but the schedule works for us. Plan your own schedule according to what will work for you.

How do I hold a family meeting? If you've never had a meeting before, casually discuss the idea with your children. Don't ask their permission (remember, you are the parent), but explain why you think it's a good idea to organize one. Keep it positive. Don't say, "I'm tired of doing everything around here. So we're going to have a family meeting to divvy up the chores!" I guarantee no one will be enthusiastic to attend. Instead, say, "I'd like us to sit down and talk about how we can better work together as a family. I have some exciting ideas and I know you will, too." Then prepare an actual written agenda. It doesn't have to be anything fancy. If your children are young, just tell them about it the night before and keep the subjects to a minimum. If your children are seven years old or older, you can be a little more formal and specific. The agenda might be typed or simply written on a piece of notebook paper posted on the refrigerator. Here's an example:

Family meeting: Thursday night after dinner
Let's talk about:
 Vacation ideas this summer
 How we can smooth the morning rush hour
 How we can get along with each other better
 Learning new household skills
 New allowance plan
 Other subjects (please write in your ideas below):
See you there!

Notice the agenda starts with a fun subject (vacation ideas) and ends with a positive one as well (allowance plan). Don't start the meeting off with your pet peeves or complaints about toothpaste in the sink. It's important that everyone get off to a positive, and respectful, start.

The first meeting will be a little awkward, but don't let it discourage you. If you continually reinforce the importance of their participation, your children will eventually appreciate the opportunity to say how they feel in a constructive setting.

Once your family gets used to the family meeting concept (usually after about three or four meetings), you can begin to get more creative. I had a problem once with my kids insulting one another. I'm sensitive to how name calling can really harm one's self-esteem and I wanted to teach them to think more positively about each other. So, once at the beginning of a family meeting, I had each of us write down three positive qualities, and one not-so-good trait, about everyone at the table. The idea was to give each of us a shot in the arm, yet openly talk about ways we could improve. That was the meeting when both my kids said I needed to watch my occasional colorful language. Apparently, they didn't think it was fair that I could use expletives when I was angry at the car breaking down or the Christmas tree falling over while they weren't permitted to show their tempers in such a manner. I grinned and said I would do my best to be more careful where my temper was concerned. What we all learned in that meeting was to praise where praise is due and to speak honestly if something bothers us.

The reason family meetings are so effective is, they give us a chance to express ourselves in a controlled, nonthreatening environment. It's so much easier to talk calmly about our feelings when we're not caught up in the anger of the moment. The next time you're tempted to scream about the kids not doing their homework or going to bed on time, stop yourself. Write down your feelings and save them for a family meeting when you can calmly talk about the consequences.

Below are other guidelines for holding effective family meetings. This list is not exhaustive, nor is it cast in stone. Create the type of meeting that best fits your family's style and needs.

Family Meeting Guidelines

- Keep attitudes light before the meeting. If you or one of the children have had a particularly rough day and don't think you can keep your composure during the meeting, it's better to postpone than to lose your cool. Kids will invariably try to turn family meetings into fighting matches. You must be in the frame of mind to control the situation calmly and positively.
- Hold your meeting in a quiet atmosphere. Turn off televisions and radios. Unplug the telephone. Ask neighbors or friends to leave. Don't let anything distract you. Sit around the kitchen table or more informally in the den or family room.
- Make sure everyone has a piece of paper and a pencil to write down what

is discussed. Your job is to facilitate the meeting, not to be the secretary. Ideally, make up notebooks for everyone before the meeting starts, so they can keep their notes of all meetings in the same place. Children are more likely to remember and adhere to ideas and concepts when they've taken the time to write them down. Encourage this as much as possible during the meeting.

- Listen to everyone. Make sure each person participates without feeling ignored or belittled. Give everyone time to initiate ideas, actions, and solutions. Bite your tongue when listening to complaints. It's important children get their feelings out, even if they seem totally off the wall or disrespectful. After they are done venting, respond calmly and reasonably. Eventually, by your example, they will learn to give the same respect you give to them.

- Make sure everyone understands what has been agreed upon before the meeting ends. For example, if everyone has decided Amanda will take out the garbage this month and Ryan will do the vacuuming, reconfirm that before the meeting ends to make sure there are no misunderstandings.

- Set a time for the next meeting to take place.

Step #4
Implement family meetings.

- Hold meetings regularly, as needed (weekly, monthly, quarterly).
- Keep meetings calm, positive, and in a quiet setting.
- Develop listening, speaking, and problem-solving rules, and stick to them during every meeting.

Teaching Household Skills

Family meetings will foster teamwork in the family, but household skills will be the real training ground where your kids will learn many important aspects of your value system. Before you can teach these skills, you must remember to

- have proper materials close by

- teach by demonstration
- stay calm and patient
- start simple and move toward more difficulty

Make sure your kids know where to get the materials they need. If you keep the cleanser under the bathroom cabinet, show them where it is. Since we remember only about 10 percent of what we hear, 50 percent of what we see, and 90 percent of what we do, it makes sense to first explain what you're going to teach, give a demonstration, then allow the child to perform the task. It will be easy for you to explain and demonstrate. The toughest part will be allowing your child to do it. If your child makes a mistake, don't draw attention to it. Calmly guide him or her in the right way. Stay with your child until you are sure he or she can do it alone. Then walk away and allow learning to take place.

It is crucial that you communicate to your child what your standards are. If you expect the bathroom counters, toilet, carpet, and tub to be spotless, say so. Don't leave it up to them to interpret what "clean the bathroom" really means. Again, I am going back to one of the first three rules: give clear directions. Praise your child for doing a good job, but don't give praise when the child has failed to comply with your standards. Calmly point out that the mirror is still a little smeary and ask for a redo. Eventually, your child will know exactly what you expect and it will be easy to interpret whether or not he or she are putting forth an honest effort or choosing to be lazy. Be patient during the learning curve. Remember, you are teaching more than a simple household chore; you are giving your child skills that he or she will take into adulthood.

When is my child old enough for certain tasks? In his book *How to be a Happy Parent . . . in Spite of Your Children!* Fred G. Gosman writes, "a child capable of programming the VCR is capable of using the washer and dryer."[7] I laughed when I read that because we often treat our children as if they are mechanically deficient, yet they usually know more about electronics and computerized gadgets than we do. It's ludicrous to think your ten-year-old can't run the vacuum cleaner or learn to use the washing machine when he or she knows exactly how to tape a favorite television show and play complicated computer games. More often, parents hesitate to teach these skills because we think we can do them better ourselves or because we know our kids will be much less enthusiastic about laundry than playing Nintendo. Don't underestimate your child's mental and physical capabilities. You will discover whether or not a child can safely perform a skill by allowing him or her to try. Showing that you trust your child and providing the opportunity for him or her to try it alone will go a long way toward building a healthy self-esteem in your child.

How do I get my children to do regular household chores? Repeatedly having to remind them makes you responsible for their behavior, not them. If you've taken the time to teach appropriately and have given enough encouragement to foster pride in a job well done, you have won half the battle. The other half is combating common, childhood procrastination. Try setting the guidelines so that household duties must be finished before any other activities, like playing with friends or watching television. Some parents feel comfortable giving their kids a window of time and letting them decide where to fit chores in the schedule. If neither of these methods are successful for you, try having a time set aside for family clean-up. Turn on some upbeat music and make a game of it. Go from room to room with them and make it a family affair.

Be creative and adjust the guidelines to your children's ages and interests. Remember, the goal of getting children to comply with household skills is to teach teamwork and foster healthy self-esteem. When you must resort to screaming, nagging, or doing it yourself, you are no longer teaching; you're taking back the responsibilities you've worked hard to turn over to your kids.

Should I pay my child to do these skills? Children are not naturally motivated by money. Our society's obsession with money is a learned behavior. Therefore, it doesn't make a lot of sense to offer to pay a child to perform household chores if they have the option to not do them for nothing. For children, learning household skills should have nothing to do with earning money, and everything to do with belonging to a family system and feeling pride and accomplishment in performing a skill. They will learn soon enough to work for money. Let this be a time when they are responsible for doing their part simply because they're a working member of the group.

Now, that's not to say that giving an allowance is a bad idea. A regular allowance will help a child learn how to be responsible with money. It's also not a bad idea to offer special jobs as an incentive for children to earn extra money in case they are saving for something special. However, don't confuse household skills with money management. Keep regular household skills separate from a monetary allowance. No one is going to pay them to do the dishes when they're on their own.

There are other things you can do to show your appreciation for your kids' participation and to offer an incentive without involving a paycheck. When my kids were young (five to seven), I had a grab bag full of small, inexpensive toys I bought at a discount store. Every week after their jobs were finished, they got to pick something from the grab bag. As they got older, I took them out for ice cream or a movie once in a while to show my appreciation. Occasional positive reinforcement was all they needed. Annie, a single mom of a three-and-a-half-year-old, uses a sticker system to get her son to pick up toys. If he earns five stickers in each of four different areas, Annie rewards him with a new toy. This may seem like a bribe, but to a young child, it's a good way to learn that helping mom will bring a reward for himself. "He really does love it," says Annie, "and I make a big production out of it." The key is in finding a reward that fits your child's age and interests.

As children grow older, it becomes appropriate to set up a cash allowance system to teach money management. My children are old enough to appreciate the value of money, and they each have special things they want to save for. The allowance system I have set up pays them every two weeks, regardless of how much work they've done around the house. If they deposit their "paycheck" into a savings account, I double their pay (with rules governing how long they must keep the money in the account). Otherwise, they get the specified amount in cash. Before they ever get paid, however, they have to submit a note to me in writing asking to be paid and whether or not they want to save or spend that week. This puts the total responsibility on them to mark paydays on their calendars, make a formal request (because I would probably forget), and decide what to do with the money (save or spend). It has worked well because there is no arguing about who did more work and who deserves more money (the two are not related), or whether or not mom remembered to pay a month ago. Their allowance is something I agree to pay them for being a positive part of the family system.

Step #5
Teach household skills.

- Choose those that are appropriate for your child's age and skill level.
- Teach by instruction, demonstration, and performance.
- Clearly communicate your standards. Praise for a job well done; otherwise, ask for a redo.
- Give incentives for family team members, but keep allowances separate from household skills.

Level Five:
The Effects of Building the First Four Levels

Once you have successfully implemented a strong family meeting and household skills plan, you will undoubtedly notice the direct impact these skills have on your child's levels of creativity, independence, and industry. Encouraging new ideas and open communication through family meetings provides a fertile environment for your kids' creativity. As a result, they will feel free to suggest better ways to run the family system and will learn to appreciate constructive criticism.

Similarly, independence and industry are two important qualities you promote when you help your kids learn basic household skills. Kids who go off to college without knowing how to do their own laundry or prepare their favorite recipes have been shortchanged by their parents and will tend to be dependent on someone else for their basic needs. Giving your kids the opportunity to learn new skills, and encouraging them to improve their efficiency and effectiveness along the way, will be an excellent foundation for any vocation they will pursue as adults.

The Final Goal: Respect

As we've worked through the pyramid, we've discussed actions, results, concepts, and values, in a systematic approach. Like any other complicated system, however, there is really not a distinct point where one level ends and the next begins.

The levels are permeable: each is interwoven with the others as you go through the process of developing an effective parenting plan.

A common theme running through each level, and ultimately completing the pyramid, is teaching respect for others and self. Vital to our children's success is an ability to balance consideration for others with that for themselves in making life choices. It is this balance that may keep them from breaking laws, abusing others, or engaging in self-destructive behavior. Yes, your kids may learn to respect life the hard way by enduring many of life's trials, but you can give them a head start by placing respect at the top of your priority list in everything you say and do. That means treating your kids with the same respect you expect from them.

"You get what you give" is the old adage, and it holds true here. Think about it: If your children can begin adulthood with healthy self-respect and consideration for others, they will be well-equipped to employ a foundation of love and example for their own parenting plan, continuing with their children the positive cycle you've begun.

In a Nutshell

Not taking time to lay a solid foundation means abandoning your children to luck or fate. Effective discipline is not about maintaining control of children, but about teaching them to control their own lives. A good discipline plan enforced over a large span of a child's life should equip them with wings to fly, not chain them to the ground. Your love, example, and patience will lay the final blocks of success to the parenting pyramid.

As Fred Gosman puts it, "When you discipline effectively, you rarely need to discipline."[8] Choose to take a proactive parenting approach, thinking through your words or actions before you react. Have a plan and stick to it. Most of us don't think twice about spending $10.95 every few months for an oil change to protect our car against major engine damage. In a similar way, a good discipline plan can protect our children from the many dangers and pressures they will face on the road to adulthood.

Don't hold your breath and hope things will turn out for the best. Seize control and train your kids by giving them love and a good example. Some day, as they drive away toward college or an independent life, you can breathe a sigh of relief, knowing you gave them the life skills they needed to face the world with confidence.

Checkpoint

- Are you more aware of how your kids interpret your words and actions?
- Have you committed to a proactive parenting approach?
- Are you beginning to identify your parenting strengths and weaknesses?
- Are you ready to accentuate your positive skills and ask for help with those you're unsure about?
- Have you had your first successful family meeting?
- Are learning and performing household skills a regular part of your family's life?
- Have you set clear boundaries for your kids, and are you prepared to enforce them?
- Are you able to consistently implement, clearly communicate, and realistically follow through with your new discipline plan?

If you can answer yes to all these questions, go on to chapter 8.

8

ENSURING YOUR CHILD'S FUTURE WELFARE

Making the decision to have a child—it's momentous. It is to decide forever to have your heart go walking around outside your body.

—Elizabeth Stone

Hope Beyond the Pain

Sheri has three children. Her son Nicholas was born when Sheri was only sixteen—he's now eleven. After a brief marriage, she and Nicholas's father divorced. Her second child, four-year-old Matheux, was fathered by an emotionally abusive alcoholic she was living with at the time. Not wanting to expose herself or her children to an increasingly bad situation, Sheri abandoned the relationship. Larissa, two, Sheri's third child, was born as a result of date rape. "That's the last time I went on a date," Sheri says. "Simply put, the circumstances leading up to my becoming a single parent three times were a result of making poor choices."

Unlike many women in her situation, Sheri accepts herself "as is," and does not regret the lessons she's learned or the opportunity to raise three beautiful children. "I don't let myself have feelings of regret. Although my relationships weren't ideal, I can't really regret them, because I have my children. They are the best things that ever happened to me. I honestly think they are very well adjusted in spite of what some may think is a less-than-perfect situation. They can never be anywhere else on this earth and be more loved or better taken care of than with me."

Sheri says her third pregnancy was a challenge because of the way her daughter was conceived. However, she says she now knows that, despite the pain, her decision to keep her child was the right one.

"I was going to give the baby up for adoption, but I knew it was a girl, and I'd always wanted a girl. So I asked myself if I would equate her with her father in ten years, or if it was more likely that I would feel something was missing from my life if I gave her up. As I am not one to go through life saying 'I wish I would have,' or 'I should have,' I knew what the right decision for me would be."

"Although the pregnancy was tough," Sheri continues, "and I can't say I felt the way I wanted to about her while I was pregnant, I knew the moment I saw her I would love her dearly. And I was right. From the moment I laid eyes on my precious baby girl, I have not regretted my decision for a moment."

Sheri recounts the time she felt vindicated from the pain her daughter's father had brought to their lives. "Here's some poetic justice. In December 1994, the year Larissa was born, her father accidentally cut off two and a half of his fingers. Since I never saw him after that first horrible night, I had a lot of anger and could never release it toward him like I wanted. Knowing he had lost a part of himself seemed justifiable in light of what he had put me through."

Now that her anger is behind her, Sheri has a renewed spirit about taking care of her responsibilities as a single parent. "No one will ever cause me to lose my dreams, ideals, and hopes for the future. I will succeed, for myself and for my children."

Making a living for her family on a secretary's salary can be trying at times, but Sheri says the real challenge comes in finding the delicate balance that it often takes a healthy, two-parent family to achieve.

"Being one person doing a two-person job is the toughest obstacle. I get up in the morning, get myself and my children ready, go to school, go to daycare, work for nine hours, pick up all the kids, go to the store (if I have to), go home and make dinner, work out, clean up the house—everyday, all by myself. If there is an activity at school or daycare, we go. If there are two in one night, we try to go to both. There is never a break. I am always the only person my children have to rely on. My children are secure in me. My children know their mother loves them, first and foremost, and will always be there for them."

Sheri says she gets some child support from Nicholas's father and has child support orders against the other two fathers, both of whom ignore them. Altogether, Sheri estimates she is missing out on $800 per month in court-ordered support.

"Without the ability to pay an attorney, relying on the state is the only way to go after child support," she says. "It is a frustrating process, but one I take very seriously. If all the support came in that was supposed to, things would get much better for us. I wouldn't have to work so much, and a lot of the stress would be gone."

Sheri says if she lost her job, she would have to go on unemployment immediately and probably apply for food stamps. "I don't rely on child support—it's too risky. I hate to say it, but we're always living on the edge financially."

Sheri makes it a point to talk to her kids about the importance of being financially responsible. "My kids know how hard it is without that extra support. They know they have to do without because there just isn't enough to go around. But mostly they know how much they miss having a father, and I believe they will carry that knowledge with them into adulthood, and hopefully be there for their children. It is something that we talk about often. They know firsthand that children suffer when a parent doesn't share in the responsibility."

According to Sheri, making education a top priority in her household helps her family look to the future with confidence. In addition to her associate's degree in interior design and technical secretarial training, Sheri is always looking to further her education.

"An education has allowed me to support my family, has kept me independent, and has fulfilled my need to learn. Education is the most important ingredient for my family's future success. In fact, my oldest son is determined to go to Harvard. We will find a way for him to get there, because I don't let any of my kids think they can't go far. Children need to be told the only thing standing in their way is the walls they build themselves. My kids all know money is tight for us and that they will be able to bypass a lot of these financial problems if they take their education seriously."

Jokingly, Sheri says her biggest accomplishment as a single parent is the same as her biggest obstacle—"waking up every morning!

"Seriously, knowing that my children are secure and happy helps me see this situation as a success story. I do a better job than a lot of two-parent families, so I see raising good kids on my own as a big accomplishment. Having children is a lifelong commitment. I knew that from the beginning, and I'm sticking to it."

❀❀❀❀❀❀❀❀❀

On any given day, 100,000 children are without a home. Every fifty-three minutes a child dies because of poverty (10,000 in a year). Every eight seconds a child drops out of school. Every sixty-seven seconds a teenager has a baby (472,623 in a year). Every seven minutes a child is arrested for a drug offense (76,986 a year), and every thirty-six minutes a child is arrested for drunken driving (17,675 a year).[1]

More than 1 million children in the United States are affected by divorce each year. An astounding one in four children in America live with only one parent. Approximately 18 million children live in mother-only households. Of the 10 million households without fathers present, two-thirds (67 percent) receive no child support and 36 percent (3.6 million) live below the poverty level.[2]

Research shows that single-mother families are vulnerable not just to poverty, but to welfare dependency. In fact, until recent welfare reform was passed by Congress, almost 40 percent of mothers who never married and received welfare remained on the rolls for ten years or longer. Additionally, welfare dependency tends to be passed on from one generation to the next. And since there is a clear connection between poverty and juvenile delinquency, it follows that the children of single-parent families are particularly vulnerable. Moreover, an alarming 70 percent of all juveniles in state reform institutions in this country come from fatherless homes.[3]

These statements and statistics are about children—children at risk. As disturbing as they are, they affect each and every one of us in one way or another. As a single parent, I remember taking exception to the grim statistics I heard about the risks my children were facing merely because they were members of a fatherless home. I believed I could overcome the numbers, and I was fortunate enough to have the resources and opportunities to educate myself and pass on the importance of education to my kids. Because of this, I hope they have been afforded a better chance to be more than I had an opportunity to be.

This chapter is about more than ensuring your children have the financial resources to live and prosper as adults. This chapter is about welfare—yours, your children's, and that of the generations to come. Steps have to be taken now to break the cycles of poverty and juvenile delinquency. Although single parents should not be blamed for the dismal conditions in which many of their children are living, they need to recognize their responsibility in changing the course of social welfare, poverty, and delinquency in America. The hardships of single parenthood cannot and should not be used as an excuse to keep children at risk.

With these things in mind, the goal in this chapter is to take what you have learned so far to a higher level, giving your children a better chance to survive in this competitive and unforgiving world. What can you do to ensure that their welfare, and the welfare of their children, is protected in the years to come? To start, take your personal growth seriously. Your commitment to career, education, financial well-being, and effective parenting will be a good foundation for a successful single-parent family. The next step is to address your children's future through planning your estate wisely, enforcing child support aggressively, choosing appropriate daycare, making good decisions, and encouraging your child's job or college prospects.

What If Something Happened to You?

Death. None of us likes to think about it. Many of us rarely do. Yet it can be one of the worst tragedies to hit a single-parent family. What would happen to your children if you were to die suddenly? Who would care for them? Would your family be left with your debt? Do you have enough life insurance to handle burial expenses and maintain your children's lifestyle until the legalities are settled? If your answer to these questions is "I don't know," then you need to pay close attention to the next few paragraphs.

Most issues of child custody after death are controlled by individual state laws, especially those of so-called tutorship or guardianship, according to Robert Levy, an assistant district attorney for family support in Louisiana. "In Louisiana, for example, the other parent is the preferred parent to have physical custody, or tutorship, because parents are tutors of their children by virtue of the parent-child relationship," he says. "It is different for legitimate and illegitimate children. Our state has established a tier of tests, i.e., the other parent, if willing and available; the grandparents, if the parent is unwilling or unable; the siblings and relatives, if none of the above; and finally, any other interested party. The state would not automatically seize control of the children." Each state will be different, so you need to know your state's guardianship laws and plan accordingly.

The bigger issue is the property of the children, or the deceased's estate. Some states allow designation of a tutor of the property, which is a separate issue from the tutor of the person. Therefore, it's wise to plan for both. The will or testament of the deceased is definitely considered but never controlling, according to Levy.

"This can be a fight at times," he says. "Unfortunately, there is little you can do to prevent an unwanted parent from gaining custody or tutorship upon your death. It's like a custody battle all over again. But you can protect the child's property and/or make the custodial parent report how the property is being used to benefit the child."

Take some time to inquire about tutorship or custodial laws in your state. Then make decisions about how you would like your property to be executed upon your death and what the stipulations would be if your ex were to be put in control of the property. Consult an attorney or other qualified professional about how to make a will. It's a fairly simple, straightforward process.

Also, analyze your life insurance situation and buy additional policies if necessary for your peace of mind. Life insurance bought through your employer is probably a good value, but shop around and find out what types of insurance will best fit your needs. An inexpensive term life policy will buy a large amount of insurance on your life and substantial amounts on your kids. Talk to an insurance professional about your options. Although there are no guarantees about what will happen to your children after you are gone, you have a better chance of making sure their needs are met if you take measures now to plan ahead for them.

Another unplanned event that could devastate your family is if you were to become disabled. You might think you're invincible, but the truth is, many things could happen that would hinder your ability to make a living. Find out through your current employer if disability benefits are part of your total benefit package. If not, you may want to consider purchasing additional insurance to guarantee at least a partial salary in the event you become incapacitated for any reason. Being unable to work and draw a paycheck for as little as thirty days could put your financial welfare at risk. Don't take the chance. Talk to your employer or an insurance professional today.

Step #1
Plan for the unexpected.

- Analyze and adjust your life and disability insurance.
- Know what will happen to the money to ensure that your children get the maximum benefit from it.
- Consult an attorney or handbook about preparing your will.

Child Support Enforcement: Myths and Realities

Child support collection is a complicated and emotional issue. Contrary to popular stereotypes, there are deadbeat moms just like deadbeat dads. There are mothers who misuse their regular child support just as there are mothers like Sheri who would use it wisely if they could only get it. There are those who abuse and use the system, and there are law-abiding parents who want to do the right thing. Although generalizing this issue would do it a disservice, the failure to mention some important misconceptions would do our children an even greater injustice.

I get letters every week from single parents who don't want to "rock the boat" by enforcing child support orders, or they don't want to take money from the other parent, fearing he or she will force the issue of visitation rights. The reasoning in both cases is neither practical nor factually based; it's merely motivated by fear.

"Sometimes it's just easier to let them off the hook than to have to deal with the anger and harassment, or, worse yet, their presence in your children's lives," said one single mom. "I'd rather not have to deal with him. I can make it without his money."

Surprisingly, this level of thinking is representative of thousands of single parents' "out of sight, out of mind" philosophy. The problems associated with this reasoning, however, reach far beyond an individual family's financial future. In fact, the social implications are mind-boggling. Statistics show that of the 10 million single-mother households in this country, 6.7 million live without child support payments. If each of these households could manage to collect $100 per month from noncustodial parents, the burden on taxpayers would be reduced by more than half a billion dollars per month! When you say no to collecting child support, you are not only depriving your child of a better lifestyle, you and others like you are collectively imposing a massive burden on society.

Even if you are functioning well without the additional help, you are nevertheless sacrificing something by not enforcing a child support order. For example, if you genuinely do not need the money to survive, you could save that $100 a month for your child's education or future welfare. Look at it this way: $100 per month saved in a mutual fund over a period of seventeen years (from infancy to college age), earning 10 percent interest, would net $53,226. That could be a formidable start on a college career, or even a decent down payment on a first home. Before deciding that you don't need the money, or deciding that your child doesn't need the money, think twice about the implications. Also, although you may not see the need for the money now, a minor financial setback or tragedy could cause you and your children to resort to public assistance later on.

The bottom line is, it is your child's right to receive financial support from parents who are capable of earning a living. Regardless of what your ex-partner tells you, child support is an obligation, not an option. And regardless of what you think, or what others tell you, child support and custody issues are completely separate from one another. A parent who does not pay child support could still have custody or visitation rights. Likewise, a parent who pays regular child support could have limited or no visitation rights, for a variety of reasons. Don't confuse the two issues. Consult an attorney or legal department before making a misguided decision.

Bringing a child into the world takes two people. Raising a child requires the financial support of both. Unfortunately, many single parents see no prospect of improving their status because of lack of child support, daycare options, and education. If you are one of these parents, take steps today to find out how you can help your state welfare office enforce your child support order. If you are unable to locate your ex-partner or need to create a child support order by establishing paternity, contact your local district attorney's office of family support. Most county agencies will help you locate your ex and even establish paternity for a nominal fee.

Step #2
Obtain the financial support your kids deserve.

- Work with local authorities to help locate your ex-partner.
- If you don't already have one, establish a child support order through your local district attorney's office.
- If you don't need it for daily expenses, invest your monthly child support.

Child Care — Every Single Parent's Nightmare

Inadequate child care is one of the most controversial and political topics being debated in this country today. It is included in this chapter because how your young children spend their time out of your care will have an enormous impact on how well they perform, both socially and academically, in the future. Some question how welfare mothers can improve their lifestyles when affordable quality daycare is out of reach. Others bemoan our children being raised by daycare providers and suggest there should be more family-oriented policies to help mothers stay at home, where their children can thrive in a home environment.

This controversy will always be with us. Ask any single parent what he or she thinks about daycare, and you will most likely hear a groan of dissatisfaction coupled with a look of bewilderment. Most often there aren't any discussions with them about whether or not daycare is good or bad for their children. All they know is that, to survive, they must rely on someone else to help care for their young children while they earn a living.

In light of this fact, the following are a few suggestions about choosing daycare and how to ensure your child is getting the most from a childcare situation.

157

- Community resource and referral agencies: These agencies will be able to provide you with a multitude of free information regarding licensed individuals and facilities, as well as recommend a situation that works best for your needs. Call 1-800-424-2246 to find the one serving your area.
- Once you have names of possible daycare candidates, call each of them to get some basic information: How long have they been in business? How many children do they care for daily? What are the hours of operation? Are the providers trained in child development and first aid? What happens when a child gets sick or hurt? What is their holiday schedule? How much do they charge?
- Obviously, the next step is to visit the facility. Don't ever make a decision based on a phone interview. Don't just visit for a few minutes, either. Stay an hour or two. When you visit, take notes on general cleanliness, available play space for each child, smells (is there an aroma of dirty diapers in the air?) and sounds (are there unattended children crying?), and the activities children are engaged in. Ask detailed questions: Do providers wash their hands after each diaper change? What types of food are served daily? How are disputes resolved between children? What happens when a child does not obey a caregiver?
- Next, analyze the schedule of activities. Look for periods of active play, quiet play, snacks and meals, and educational activities. According to the National Association for the Education of Young Children (NAEYC), there should be no more than eight babies in a group, with one adult assigned for every four infants. They also recommend no more than twelve kids per group for toddlers (twelve to thirty months old), with one adult assigned to every four younger toddlers and one adult to every six older toddlers.
- Ask the center director or home provider for references and check them out. If staff members seem apprehensive about it or say they don't have any, beware. Most good providers will have a long list of people who are willing to serve as references.
- For school-age children, look for after-school care that is educational and interesting. This is the age when your children will need more than a baby-sitter. Many after-school programs, which are often held in elementary

school gymnasiums, are affordable, but be cautious. Look for a reliable and qualified staff, a variety of activities and materials, a pleasant and safe environment, facilities for active play as well as for doing homework quietly, and good adult supervision with clear-cut safety policies intact.

• Before deciding to leave your school-age child to fend for him- or herself after school or on weekends, think long and hard about how that will impact his growth and what risks are involved. Structured and planned activities are important for youths to keep them involved in mind-expanding rather than self-destructive activities. Don't kid yourself: a kid with too little to do will find something to do. Take steps to control what that something might be by investing the time and money to research the possibilities. Boys and girls clubs are in many communities. Safe-key programs and after-school activities abound.

Step #3
Make childcare choices a priority.

• Investigate possibilities thoroughly.
• Call each prospect and ask basic questions.
• Visit facilities or homes to get a true feel for daily activities.
• Don't leave a school-age child with no after-school plan.

Making Choices: We Reap What We Sow

More astonishing than the letters from parents who are afraid to collect child support are the letters from parents who continue to make poor decisions despite their hardships, yet want to place the blame on someone else. Now, I'm the last person to judge anyone for having made a serious mistake or two in life. Those of us who have endured divorce realize the negative impact a poor relationship choice can make on a family. But to expect others to take responsibilities that you yourself are not willing to assume is asking too much.

Consider your own reaction when you read about the following occurrences:

- a welfare mother who continues to have babies despite her dire financial state
- a dad who keeps fathering children without paying any child support
- a teen who again gets pregnant after having her sixth abortion
- a parent who blows his or her paycheck on drugs or alcohol

Most people feel anger, even disgust, when they read or hear about such things happening because they know these people are acting foolishly and are endangering children in the process. Worse yet, they know some portion of their tax dollars are funding this foolishness and irresponsibility.

Without getting into the political debate surrounding these issues, suffice it to say, everyone makes mistakes. And anyone can make a bad decision. After all, no one knows what he or she would do in a particular situation until that situation presents itself. But somewhere along the line, these people have abused their freedom of choice. These days, "if it feels good, do it" seems to reign over asking, "What if?" If you truly care about the future health and welfare of your children, take a moment to examine how and why you make decisions. In most cases, the law of nature that we reap what we sow holds true, so let's begin sowing seeds of wisdom for our children.

Step #4
Respect your freedom to make choices, but start with good decisions.

- Consider how the small decisions you make today will affect your child's future.
- Commit to providing your child with opportunities and choices.
- Hold yourself to the same moral standards you expect from others.

Your Child's Future Job Prospects

Economically, too many young people are confronted with only two choices in terms of work: a limited number of professional, often high technology possibilities, or a world of relatively low-income service jobs—McDonalds, the proverbial "mickeyDs," is the metaphor. The blue collar positions that were the avenue to the suburbs for millions of Americans after World War II have shrunk precipitously.[4]

Peter B. Edelman and Joyce Ladner penned these poignant words about what our kids can expect from the job market going into the twenty-first century. We can no longer encourage our children to go after a secure factory job and expect to hold it for thirty years until retirement. Skilled labor is quickly being replaced with high-tech computer equipment, and if you expect your children to get all they need from high school to thrive and prosper as adults, you're kidding yourself. In the coming century, a high school education will only be a stepping stone to a college career.

To a large degree, that is already the case. It doesn't matter what you did in 1978, or what your Uncle Joe did in 1952. The reality now is that the higher-paying jobs of the twenty-first century will be those that require a specialized education. Kids with only a general high school background will find low-paying employment, and those who drop out of high school will take whatever is left.

Getting a good education doesn't mean getting a degree from Yale or Harvard. There is a college, university, or technical school out there for every child's financial and vocational needs. Your children were not born with the knowledge or information needed to make good career decisions, however. You must instill the importance of education in them. That means taking time to gather information about job prospects and college institutions, learning about your children's interests and aptitudes, encouraging activities to help them perfect their skills, and encouraging learning in your everyday life.

Maybe you didn't go to college. Maybe you didn't even graduate from high school. Don't shy away from talking about education simply because you don't know anything about it. A few phone calls to a few colleges or universities will be enough to at least obtain some pamphlets or catalogs to help you learn about the process. Don't wait until your son or daughter is threatening to drop out of high school before you take action. Start early. Most libraries carry comprehensive college guides that list names of major colleges and universities, and what types of degrees and fields of study they offer. Check one out and take it home to read to your kids. They love adventure stories. What better adventure than to talk about where they might travel to college someday and what interesting careers they might encounter along the way. If you can dream with them, you give them permission to dream on their own.

Step #5
Help your child plan early for career choices.

- Inform yourself about the possibilities and prospects.
- Get your kids involved in the dreaming process.
- Encourage them to be the best they can be.

In a Nutshell

We've got to stop thinking that tragedy will never happen, that our kids will automatically grow up to be better off than we are, and that it's someone else's responsibility to see to our welfare. It's time to take control—not only of our own lives, but of the welfare of generations to come. We've got to stop giving birth to more children than we can take care of, or expecting our kids to be anything better than we're willing to be ourselves. It's time to take an active part in helping our kids plan for their education and job prospects. It's time to care about the future.

It's a tall order. When we consider the morally deficient state of our country and the general here-and-now attitudes of its people, it may seem that we have already waited too long to turn the tables around in favor of our kids. But maybe with a little awareness and a concerted effort to take charge of our own affairs, our kids just might have a chance for a more prosperous and self-fulfilling existence. Start today, in your home, to ensure your children a good future.

Checkpoint

- Have you talked to someone about life or disability insurance?
- Are you prepared to write your will?
- Do you feel comfortable that your children will be taken care of adequately in the event of your death?
- Have you inquired about getting a child support order?
- Have you thought about what you might do with child-support payments to benefit your children's lives and future welfare?
- Have you investigated all childcare possibilities and made a choice you are comfortable with?
- Are you ready to commit to good decision-making?
- Have you investigated college and career prospects for your children?
- Are you encouraging your kids to dream about the future?

If you can answer yes to all these questions, go on to chapter 9.

9

GIVING YOUR CHILD THE BEST CHANCE FOR SUCCESS

If you have made mistakes . . . there is always another chance for you
. . . you may have a fresh start any moment you choose, for this thing
we call failure is not the falling down, but the staying down.

—Mary Pickford

A True Labor of Love

When Terry was barely twenty-five years old, she had no idea motherhood was looming around the corner for her. Most women have several months to prepare themselves for the task, but in Terry's case it was only a matter of days. One summer day in Pennsylvania fourteen years ago, a family's vacation was shattered by tragedy: Terry's younger sister and her sister's husband were killed in an automobile accident. It was an event that would forever change the course of Terry's life. The deceased couple's two young daughters, ages four and two, were injured but survived the ordeal. The girls were left without their parents to comfort them— but Terry, unmarried and with her whole life ahead of her, stepped in to take over as their surrogate mother and caretaker.

"Becoming a parent of two at twenty-five was tough, but I was the big sister," remembers Terry. "There really was no choice in my mind. It was just something I had to do for my sister, and I loved the girls dearly."

165

Now at age thirty-nine, Terry proudly talks about her two teenage honor students. She says that despite a series of facial plastic surgeries each of the girls had to undergo after the accident, her daughters are "very well-adjusted and ready to take on the world.

"Just about everything I have done in my life since the accident has been centered around them," she says. "I sent them to parochial schools and kept a tight reign on them, trying not to be too over protective. They had insurance money that was left for them after the accident that I've saved through the years. So now there is money available for them to enter college."

Crystal, eighteen, plans to attend Drexel University to study architectural engineering. Laura, now sixteen and a soon-to-be high school senior, also has plans to attend college. Terry says the toughest aspect of single parenting has been keeping the proper balance in their family.

"It's hard to be the good guy and the bad guy. I had to set and enforce the rules, but I also had to know when to let up on them once in a while. I wanted the girls to experience life, but at the same time I wanted to keep them safe."

She says she is now beginning to see the true fruits of her labor, as she watches her daughters turn into responsible young women. "I have really been blessed. Other than a few bouts with typical teenage stuff, they are very well behaved and sensible. They have good friends and no desire to drink or use drugs. Trying to let them be independent and still keep some controls has been difficult, but I really feel I have done all I can do to give them the right tools to succeed. That's all any parent can really expect from herself."

Terry says that her social life took a back seat when she became an instant mom, but now that the kids are older, she's getting out more often.

"I don't look back with any regrets," she says. "I couldn't love these kids any more if they were my natural children. The fact is, we're very different from most single-parent homes. It's been interesting dealing with the confused reactions of other adults and teachers, but it hasn't bothered the girls. They've always been very open about their parents' death."

The time when her daughters will no longer need a full-time mom is getting painfully closer, Terry says, so planning for her own future is at the top of the list these days. She's working toward an associate's degree in microcomputer processing.

"My life has centered around them for so long, that not having them as my focus is hard to imagine. I started college again last fall, hoping to fill in the gaps when the girls are no longer around.

"They really have no idea that it's a little scary for me to think about being alone again," she adds. "They're just happy to be moving on with their lives, which I think is a sign we've been doing the right things."

✱✱✱✱✱✱✱✱✱✱

Remember when you discovered you were pregnant for the first time? Whether you were excited, depressed, calm, or nervous, the next eight or nine months were a test in patience. For me, it seemed my due date would never come soon enough—and I had a premature baby at seven months. After the baby is born, there is a period of about three years when the child needs your undivided attention most of the time. Speech and coordination come slowly but surely. It seems you'll never again have a free moment to yourself.

Lo and behold, the preschool years are upon you and things begin to move a little faster. You love every stage and call it your favorite. You want every age to last a little longer, yet you're anxious to see what the next stage will bring. Learning, speaking, and doing are all at a fast pace by age four. Then comes the bittersweet day when your child starts kindergarten. A thirteen-year journey begins when a large portion of your child's day will be entrusted to other adults for guidance, learning, and discipline. Your child's friends will now be a regular influence in his or her life.

The time between your child's first day of kindergarten and high school graduation seems to happen in a flash. Life gets busier and busier with every year. Before you know it, you're saying good-bye and questioning whether you've done everything right, or whether your child has what it takes to survive. By then, you just pray and ask God to help your child remember all you've taught him or her over the years.

This chapter is different from the previous eight: I'm not going to give you a step-by-step plan to follow. Everything provided here is to challenge you, to inspire you to go beyond what others may expect of you as a parent, to encourage excellence in your vital role. What you have learned so far will be plenty to get you on the road to success. But to be truly effective, to give your children the absolute best chance for success, you must decide to give the very best you have to give.

I would like to recap a few important ideas we've discussed in this book and interject a list of suggestions that might encourage you to be the best you can be. These aren't surefire ways to lock in good parent-child relationships, by any means. But those who are willing to try them regularly will probably find they've struck a pot of gold.

- Talk (don't lecture) about values.

    In chapter 7 we talked about the importance of teaching values by example. Your guidance through verbal communication is also important. This doesn't mean regularly sitting down and having heart-to-heart talks with your children (better known as a lectures). On the contrary, the more informal, natural, and spontaneous the conversations, the better.

    Of course, being prepared at all times to discuss your values with, or in front of, your children requires you to know and understand your personal belief system and know it well, which, as we discussed earlier, requires a great deal of soul searching and a commitment to self-nurturing. You owe it to your children to teach them what you have learned. Although they will never truly understand until they have experienced their own trials, you can prepare them well by sharing your wisdom in words. Helping them to emerge from childhood with their own individual beliefs and value systems will be the best and most lasting gift you can ever hope to give.

    Take opportunities at home, during the course of your normal daily life, to talk about your values. After watching a movie or television program would be a good time to discuss the story taught and how it affirmed or contradicted your values. Likewise, when your child is having trouble with a friend at school, encourage him or her to talk about it and find ways to discuss the problem from a values standpoint. Also, give value-based reasons for your own actions and decisions. If your child disagrees with you about a curfew, explain why curfews are important; don't just say, "Because I said so." Talking about values is really not that difficult if you're confident in what you believe and you think through it.

I remember sitting around the family dinner table with my parents and talking about a variety of subjects, whatever seemed to come up at the time. Sometimes, my parents would relate stories about their childhood or ours, and we listened, much amused. Other times, we would listen to my dad, a business owner, voice his opinions on politics or what he thought were fair or unfair business practices. He never said, "Now hear this, kids. I'm about to say something important." He just talked and we listened. He probably didn't realize how much we listened to his rhetoric (maybe he would have occasionally changed his words had he known the impact!), but we listened and placed value on what he had to say. As much as I try to teach my own personal value system in my home today, I have to believe the echo of my parents' words from long ago still strongly influences my teaching.

Don't underestimate the ability of your kids to pick up on everything going on around them. Your example and your words, whether spoken to them or someone else, will be closely scrutinized, considered, and adopted by your children. Don't lecture about your belief system; live, breathe, and talk about it in your daily routine. If you want to earn respect from your children, be true to yourself. They will thank you for it in the years to come.

- Don't try to change the world; change a life or two.

We're often told that "money isn't everything," "you can't take it with you," and "the best things in life are free." As true as these sayings may be, it's also true that getting a good education and making wise career and financial choices are goals we all hope our children attain. We know how important career and financial stability are to a person's feelings of self-worth in our society. A child is not born with the need or instinct to desire monetary gain or want an academic education. Whatever thoughts he or she has on these subjects will be molded by you and the world your child lives in. Since you have the most control of what your child hears, sees, and experiences, especially in the first six years of life, begin early to instill in him or her a healthy attitude about education and finances.

- Go the extra mile.

    Sometimes we just have to take a few moments out of our busy schedules to ask ourselves what we would have wanted from our parents when we were growing up. More than likely, we can come up with a few simple answers. And even more likely, those answers will involve just a little more time, a little more love, and a little more understanding. A little more now may save you a lot more later.

- Say "I love you" often.

    If you aren't comfortable with the words, try writing them down in a note on your children's pillow or in their lunchbag. They will become easier and easier each time you say them, so get lots of practice. You can't say them too much, but you can say them too little.

- Give a hug at least every day.

    Research proves that positive physical contact with a loved one on a daily basis helps relieve stress. Remember, single parents need a hug every day as much as their kids do. Make sure the hug is a good strong one. It's also better when accompanied by the words "I love you."

- Compliment your child's strengths and downplay his or her weaknesses.

    Take every opportunity to encourage your child's individual talents. It may be your daughter's good handwriting or the neat way your son makes a peanut butter sandwich. Whatever your children do best, let them know you recognize and appreciate their skills. We live in a world where everything popular seems to be dictated by the media. Teach them individualism by encouraging personal skills and activities that make them feel proud and valuable.

- Eat at least one meal together every day.

    A recent study found that the only common denominator among high school National Merit Scholars was that their families regularly ate dinner together. If having dinner together regularly can produce a National Merit Scholar, can you imagine the positive effect other simple family activities might have? Eating a meal together will give you a place to talk about the problems of the day, create a feeling of belonging to something positive, and strengthen family cohesiveness.

- Pray together at the dinner table.

    This may be a real stretch for you if you have never prayed together before or if you have no religious background. Start simple. Pray the "God is good" prayer if you have to. Your kids may even laugh and think it's corny. But if you keep doing it, gradually interjecting more meaningful words such as "Thank you, Lord, for keeping our family healthy" or "Bless us with love and good health," they will unknowingly begin to respect and appreciate the presence of a higher power in their lives. Try it; it can't hurt.

- Mend your relationship with the other parent, or at least do your part.

    This is a tough one, but it is vital for fostering healthy attitudes in your household. If you are divorced, separated, or estranged from your children's other parent, chances are, you are still uncomfortable when you come in contact with him or her. Believe me, your kids are aware of this. Once the dust settles, find a common ground with your ex, especially where it concerns your children. It may not be possible to be friends, but you still need to try hard to be civil and accommodating and to maintain stability. You cannot prevent the other parent from treating you uncivilly, but you can contrast his or her behavior with your own self-control. Your kids will see the difference and respect you for trying to do your part.

    Dr. Bobbie Reed, in her article "Making Visitation Work," suggests the following to smooth a rough relationship:

    —Have the child ready on time when the other parent arrives and send along appropriate clothes and equipment.

    —Pick-up and drop-off times should never be turned into forums for arguing.

    —Be courteous toward the other parent and give as much notice as possible when plans need to change.

    —Never belittle the other parent.

    —Remember that the rules of the other household are in effect during the child's stay there, just as your rules are followed in your own home.

—Share copies of school pictures, report cards, photos, and other important information.[1]

- Speak respectfully about the other parent.

No matter how hurt you feel by the actions of your ex, you are fighting a losing battle if you think you're going to convince your children that you are the better parent. By nature, kids want to trust and love their parents equally. They are willing to forgive and forget for one more chance to find balance and feel loved again. When one parent continually berates the other, kids will often side with the victim of the verbal abuse. If the other parent truly is unworthy of your kids' trust and respect, they will discover it on their own through day-to-day experiences with him or her. Besides, you will provide a much healthier environment (and retain a great deal of respect) if you refrain from saying anything derogatory about the other parent. Just concentrate on your own efforts.

- Join a church or synagogue and attend regularly.

Single parents need all the help they can get to raise their children in a healthy environment. Church youth groups and activities will give your children an additional outlet, apart from daily school life, to interact with other kids in a controlled and value-based setting. Of course, mingling with church members does not mean you will be guaranteed trustworthy friends and acquaintances. However, chances are good that you will find good people there who have similar values and who will be interested in your family's well-being.

- Have at least three nights each week of no television.

At the risk of sounding stark-raving mad, it is a good idea to turn off the TV—ideally, every night; more realistically, at least three nights per week. My own family began this tradition after I remarried, and it has been the best reinforcement of family time together that we have ever experienced. It's amazing the activities you can find to do when television isn't an option. We've had chess tournaments, put puzzles together, made crafts. It's really very easy to replace passive TV-watching with something else. Try it for at least a month, then decide if you like it. I guarantee you will.

- Plan at least one outdoor activity together per month.

    It's easy to get in lockstep with our jobs, school activities, sports events, and so forth, and forget how important it is to get out and experience nature as a family. There are so many lessons to be learned from our natural surroundings. Bike riding, hiking, boating, camping, even a picnic at the park—all provide opportunities to breathe fresh air and talk about the wonders of nature (not to mention the feeling of separation from the daily stresses of life). Plan it and do it faithfully every month, and begin making wonderful family memories.

- Plant a garden together.

    There's something about tilling the soil, planting the seed, and harvesting the fruit that is extremely good for the soul. I remember planting a flower garden soon after my divorce and pulling weeds when I was angry. It was such a good release, plus I was able to really see the fruits of my effort in the long run. I was, in a sense, turning my negative energy into something productive. As I grew personally, I began to look at my garden with more pride and affection. I loved caring for my plants— watering, feeding, weeding. It was as if I was caring for my soul at the same time. Caring for a garden as a family can be a silent testimonial to your values. Without saying it specifically, you will be teaching responsibility, nurturing, and pride in accomplishment. Turning barren soil into a beautiful plant is a parallel lesson on life. Don't miss this perfect opportunity to experience growth.

- Get to know your children's friends.

    You don't have to be one of the kids to know who your children are spending time with. Pay close attention to the individuals your children choose to be their friends. Instead of criticizing how someone looks or acts, try finding out more about him or her—family situations, backgrounds, interests, and so on. Invite children's friends over for an informal dinner one evening or offer to take all of them shopping or to a school function. A casual observation might reveal you were wrong about your initial suspicions, or that you were justified in feeling apprehensive about a certain friend. Whatever you discover, taking time to find out for yourself will not only give you peace of mind, it will prove to your child that you are willing to judge a book by more than its cover.

- Visit the dentist regularly.

    Yes, that's what I said. Take care of your family's smiles! Good dental hygiene is wise and promotes confidence and self-esteem. Smiling is one of the most important tools of communication we possess. It's how we communicate pleasure and compassion, and it's how we respond to humor. Don't short-change your family by ignoring the power of a smile. A bright and healthy one can go far in our impersonal world.

- Visit the library at least twice a month.

    There's no doubt about it, reading is fundamental to everything in our lives. Most children who never learn to read well were never encouraged to be curious about books. From an early age, familiarize your children with the library and let them discover the world through books. Our library systems were built on the belief that reading is the backbone of society. Reading is free, it's fun, and it's a ticket to experience the wonders of the world without leaving home.

    Of course, encouraging your children to read goes hand in hand with visiting the library. Every evening before my kids go to sleep, I encourage them to read for at least an hour. Reading relaxes the body and leaves the mind with positive thoughts before slumber. If you're not accustomed to a reading schedule, start simple. Take turns reading a story out loud every night. Make it an easy-to-read adventure story and read a chapter a night. When you've accomplished that, the habit will have been started, and it will be easier to get your kids to read something quietly on their own. You may not understand the value of regular reading now, but eventually this will become a ritual that you will all cherish and will have fond memories of in the years to come.

- Make a point to spend planned time alone with each of your kids.

    If you only have one child, this will be easy. If you have two or more children, however, you will likely agree that this is not an easy task for a single parent. Too many times, children in single-parent families feel like they're just part of a clan, without individual worth. Single parents have a tough time spending individual moments with each child and often treat all the children the same because it's convenient and simple. The truth of the matter is, each child is different and demands a unique blend of discipline, recreation, and emotional attention.

Make it a point to schedule alone time with each of your children at least once a month. If you can't get away from the house, find a way to do something special without being interrupted by the other children. This may take some creative planning and conversation with the family about the importance of special time with Mom or Dad, but it can be done. Find out what is special about each of your children. Discover favorite foods, favorite activities, and special talents. Your children will appreciate your interest in their lives and feel encouraged by your effort to get to know them individually, and you will reap the rewards of having children who are not always competing for your attention.

In a Nutshell

What is success? Ask any two people and you will get two different answers. The trouble with measuring success in something as complicated as parenting is that you never really know when you've completed the "something" you've set out to accomplish! Parenting is an ongoing maze of isolated problems and trial-and-error solutions, a roller coaster ride of regrets and rewards, and a lifetime responsibility with a distinct beginning but a clouded end. Because good parenting is in part a learned skill, quite often we only truly know if we have completed our job when our children manage to succeed as parents themselves.

A good single-parenting rule of thumb to live by is this: if you can raise a family on your own, achieve personal goals along the way, teach valuable lessons with lasting effects, and look back with limited regrets—knowing you did everything in your power to bring balance and meaning to your child's fragile life—you, my friend, will have achieved success. Happy parenting!

APPENDIX

Worksheet A
Financial — The Tangibles

What is my net worth?

ASSETS:
> Cash and bank accounts
> > (savings, checking, cash on hand, etc.) _____

> Market value of residence _____

> Market value of automobiles _____

> Other Assets
> > (personal belongings, other real estate, etc.) _____

> Investments
> > (stocks, bonds, profit sharing, 401k plans, etc.) _____

TOTAL ASSETS (+) _____

LIABILITIES:
> Credit cards
> > (Visa, MasterCard, gasoline cards,
> > department store cards, etc.) _____

> Other loans
> > (bank loans, lines of credit, personal loans) _____

> Car loans _____

> Mortgage loan _____

TOTAL LIABILITIES (-) $ _____

OVERALL TOTAL (=) $ _____
(Total Assets - Total Liabilities)

Worksheet B
Spending Habits/Priorities Analysis

How do I spend my money?

Use your checkbook, sales receipts or consult your memory to fill in amounts for each category.

In the last thirty days, how much did you spend on

Daycare? _____

Food (bought at the grocery store)? _____

Mortgage or rent? _____

Car payment? _____

Car insurance? _____

Car maintenance (gas, oil, check-ups)? _____

Other insurance (rent/homeowners, life, health)? _____

Medical expenses?

Utilities (electric, natural gas, water, sewage,

    sanitation)? _____

Telephone? _____

Cable television? _____

Credit cards? _____

Other loans and notes? _____

School tuition (kids' and yours)? _____

Lunches (kids' and yours)? _____

Kids' school supplies and activities? _____

Kids' clothing? _____

Kids' allowances? _____

Your personal clothing? _____

Professional laundry or dry cleaning? _____

Family toiletries (cosmetics, deodorant, shampoo, etc.) _____

Beauty/barber shop?

Cleaning products? _____

Household goods (redecorating, maintenance, etc.) _____

Subscriptions (newspapers, magazines, book clubs)? _____

Eating out (fast food, pizza deliveries, restaurants)? _____

Entertainment (movies, amusement parks,

dates, partying)? _____

Baby-sitting? _____

Charity (donations to churches, civic groups,

nonprofits)? _____

Savings (local bank, credit unions)? _____

Investments (stocks, bonds, 401(k)/profit-sharing plans)? _____

Gifts (Christmas, birthdays, etc.) _____

Instructions: In the left margin by each category, number the amounts from highest (number 1) to lowest (number 32). You may have several categories where the amount spent is zero. Stop numbering when you get to those amounts.

Analyze your ten highest amounts and your ten lowest amounts.
- How do these expenditures coincide with your values?
- Are you spending the most money on the areas that are most important to you?
- How could you change your spending habits to better reflect your value system?

Appendix

Worksheet C
Other Assets & Liabilities — The Intangibles

What qualities do I have going for or against me?

ASSETS: (check all that apply)

I am often . . .

☐ Money-conscious   ☐ Dedicated/loyal   ☐ Charitable
☐ Spiritual   ☐ Learning new things   ☐ Healthy
☐ Intelligent   ☐ Sensible   ☐ Easy-going
☐ Compassionate   ☐ Appreciative   ☐ Respected
☐ _____   ☐ _____   ☐_____

I usually have . . .

☐ Children who love me   ☐ A comfortable home   ☐ Family values
☐ Job security   ☐ Friends who care   ☐ A positive attitude
☐ A plan for the future   ☐ A strong work ethic   ☐ A love of nature
☐ _____   ☐ _____   ☐_____

LIABILITIES

I am often . . .

☐ An impulse buyer   ☐ Unmotivated   ☐ Selfish
☐ Shallow/cold-hearted   ☐ A couch potato   ☐ Ill/sickly
☐ Making bad decisions   ☐ Foolish   ☐ A worrier
☐ Mean/untrusting   ☐ Expecting too much   ☐ Belittled by others
☐ _____   ☐ _____   ☐_____

I usually have . . .

☐ Unhappy children   ☐ Unclear values   ☐ A tense home
☐ No job/no income   ☐ Many enemies   ☐ A negative attitude
☐ No regard for nature   ☐ No desire to work   ☐ No dreams or goals
☐ _____   ☐ _____   ☐_____

Instructions: Check all the intangible assets and liabilities you feel you possess. Add others not shown here on the blank lines.

Assess your assets and liabilities.
- Do you have more assets than liabilities?
- How does each one affect your ability to earn a living?
- Are your assets and liabilities congruent with your value system?
- Would making changes (turning some liabilities into assets) have an impact on your family's future?

Make a commitment to change. List the liabilities you would like to turn into assets and give reasons why.

_____

_____

_____

_____

_____

_____

_____

_____

_____

_____

_____

_____

_____

Worksheet D
Income & Expenses

What is my current monthly cash flow?

MONTHLY INCOME

Employment: (If paid weekly, multiply amounts by 52 and divide by 12; If paid bi-weekly, multiply amounts by 27 and divide by 12)

Gross: $ _____

Minus: Taxes   - _____

           Insurance Premiums   - _____

           Other   - _____

Net take-home pay: = _____

Child Support: + _____

Other Income (alimony, rental, interest/dividend):   + _____

Total Net Income $ _____

EXPENSES

    Home (30%):

       Mortgage/Rent$ $ _____

         (Payment, interest, taxes, and insurance)

    Utilities (10%):

       Electric   _____

       Natural Gas   _____

       Telephone   _____

       Water   _____

       Sewage   _____

       Sanitation   _____

         Total Utilities $ _____

Daycare/School Expenses (15%): $ _____

Food and Personal Items (15%): $ _____

Transportation (10%):

    Car loan   _____

    Car insurance   _____

    Registration/license ($\div 12$)   _____

    Maintenance   _____

    Fuel   _____

    Bus/subway fare   _____

            Total Transportation $ _____

Medical (% varies): $ _____

Clothing (% varies): $ _____

Savings/Investment (10%): $ _____

Charity (% varies): $ _____

Optionals (10%):

    Entertainment   _____

    Dining out   _____

    Professional dry cleaning   _____

    Beauty/barber care   _____

    Subscriptions   _____

    Cable television   _____

    Other   _____

          Total Optionals $ _____

                Total Expenses $ _____

            Income - Expenses = $ _____

Instructions: Multiply expense by the percentages listed with each category (or determine your own) to get a target spending plan.

Analyze your expenses.
- Where can you cut back in order to have money in the savings category?
- How can you allocate your at-risk income to cover nonessential expenses?
- What can you do to ensure a regular savings plan?

Worksheet E
Personal Survival Network

Who can I call on in times of need?

Personal friends:
Male and female single parents, married couples, older mentors

_____ _____ _____

Phone _____ Phone _____ Phone _____

Relatives:
Parents, grandparents, sisters and brothers, aunts and uncles

_____ _____ _____

Phone _____ Phone _____ Phone _____

Professional Counselors:
Counselor, pastor, minister, rabbi, priest

_____ _____ _____

Phone _____ Phone _____ Phone _____

Health Providers:
Family physician, dentist, gynecologist, eye doctor, pharmacist, veterinarian

_____ _____ _____

Phone _____ Phone _____ Phone _____

Automobile Advisors:
Insurance agent, mechanic, automobile club representative

_____   _____   _____

Phone _____   Phone _____   Phone _____

Household Advisors:
Insurance agent, heating/cooling repairman, plumber, general repair person

_____   _____   _____

Phone _____   Phone _____   Phone _____

Financial/Legal Advisors:
Local bank representative, attorney, financial consultant

_____   _____   _____

Phone _____   Phone _____   Phone _____

General Confidants:
Daycare providers, coworker(s), post office worker, grocery store manager

_____   _____   _____

Phone _____   Phone _____   Phone _____

Instructions: Write in three names for each category and commit to contacting each of them about becoming part of your network. Make at least one contact per week. Breathe easier, knowing you have a group of people you can count on.

Worksheet F
Expectations/Consequences

Do I know what I expect of my children?

SPIRITUAL MATTERS

My Expectation: _____

_____

The Consequence: _____

_____

OUTWARD APPEARANCE

My Expectation: _____

_____

The Consequence: _____

_____

SCHOOLWORK

My Expectation: _____

_____

The Consequence: _____

_____

EXTRACURRICULAR ACTIVITIES
My Expectation: _____

_____

The Consequence: _____

_____

MONEY
My Expectation: _____

_____

The Consequence: _____

_____

HOUSEHOLD SKILLS
My Expectation: _____

_____

The Consequence: _____

_____

CURFEWS
My Expectation: _____

_____

The Consequence: _____

_____

GENERAL ATTITUDE
My Expectation: _____

_____

The Consequence: _____

_____

RESPECT FOR OTHERS
My Expectation: _____

_____

The Consequence: _____

_____

RESPECT FOR PROPERTY
My Expectation: _____

_____

The Consequence: _____

_____

SELF-RESPECT
My Expectation: _____

_____

The Consequence: _____

_____

NOTES

Chapter 1

1. Shoshana Alexander, *In Praise of Single Parents* (New York: Houghton Mifflin, 1994), 3.

2. Thomas Whiteman, *The Fresh Start Single Parenting Workbook* (Nashville: Thomas Nelson Publishers, 1993), 22.

3. M. Scott Peck, *The Road Less Traveled* (New York: Simon & Schuster, 1978), 15–16.

Chapter 2

1. Paul Watzlawick, et al., *Change* (New York: W. W. Norton, 1974), 94-99.

2. Gary Richmond, *Successful Single Parenting: Going It Alone* (Eugene, Oregon: Harvest House Publishers, 1990), 32.

3. William Bridges, *Managing Transitions: Making the Most of Change* (Reading, Massachusetts: Addison-Wesley, 1991) 20, 31.

4. Shoshana Alexander, *In Praise of Single Parents* (New York: Houghton Mifflin, 1994), 284.

5. Carole Klein and Richard Gotti, *Overcoming Regret: Lessons from the Road Not Taken* (New York: Bantam, 1992), 33–34.

6. Devorah Major, "A Cord Between Us," in *The Single Mother's Companion,* ed. Marsha R. Leslie (Seattle: Seal Press, 1994), 12–15.

Chapter 3

1. Hannah Hurnard, *Hinds' Feet on High Places* (Wheaton, Illinois: Tyndale House, 1975), 66, 152.

2. Stephanie Dowrick, *Intimacy and Solitude: Balancing Closeness and Independence* (New York: W. W. Norton, 1991), 12.

3. Viktor Frankl, *Man's Search for Meaning,* 3rd ed., trans. Ilse Lasch and Gordon W. Allport (New York: Simon & Schuster, 1984), 55.

Chapter 4

1. Gordon Porter Miller, *Life Choices: How to Make the Critical Decisions— About Your Education, Career, Marriage, Family, Life* (New York: Thomas Y. Crowell, 1978), 31, 157.

Chapter 6

1. Neal Barnard, *Food for Life* (New York: Crown, 1993), 168.
2. Teddi Sanford and Mickie Padorr Silverstein, *Marrying Again* (Chicago: Contemporary Books, 1988, 173–4.

Chapter 7

1. Gregory Bodenhamer, *Back in Control* (New York: Prentice Hall, 1983), 14, 25, 41.
2. Salley Shannon, "Play Up Your Strengths," *Working Mother,* March 1995.
3. Dorothy Corkille Briggs, *Your Child's Self-Esteem* (New York: Doubleday Dell, 1970), 45-53.
4. Virginia Stowe with Andrea Thompson, "6 Easy Discipline Tips," *Working Mother,* October, 1995.
5. Malcolm W. Klein, *The American Street Gang* (New York: Oxford University Press, 1995), 78.
6. Patricia H. Sprinkle, *Do I Have To?* (Grand Rapids, Michigan: Zondervan, 1993), 73.
7. Fred G. Gosman, *How to Be a Happy Parent . . . In Spite of Your Children!* (New York: Villard Books, 1995), 63.
8. Ibid., 38.

Chapter 8

1. *Children Cope with Divorce* (Las Vegas: Child Service and Family Counseling Center, Inc., 1990).
2. M. Franco Salvoza, "Father Figures," *USA Weekend,* June 14–16, 1996, 5.
3. Robin Brown, ed., *Children in Crisis* (n.p.: H. W. Wilson, 1994), 39.
4. Peter B. Edelman and Joyce Ladner, eds., *Adolescence and Poverty: Challenge for the 1990s* (n.p.: Center for National Policy Press, 1991), 2.

Chapter 9

1. Bobbie Reed, "Making Visitation Work," *Single-Parent Family,* February 1995, 19–22.

RESOURCE GUIDE

Adoption

Committee for Single Adoptive Parents
Publishes *Handbook for Single Adoptive Parents*
P.O. Box 15084
Chevy Chase, MD 20825
(202) 966-6367

Single Parents Adopting Children Everywhere (SPACE)
6 Sunshine Avenue
Natick, MA 01760
(508) 655-5426

Single Parents With Adopted Kids (SWAK)
4108 Washington Road, Suite 101
Kenosha, WI 53144
(414) 654-0629

Adult Education

Displaced Homemakers Network
1625 K Street N.W., Suite 300
Washington, DC 20006
(202) 467-6346

An Income of Her Own
Provides teenage women with the experience and inspiration to achieve
P.O. Box 987
Santa Barbara, CA 93120
(800) 350-2978

Bureau of Labor Statistics
Division of Occupational Outlook
Washington, DC 20212-0001

Child Care

National Association for the Education of Young Children (NAEYC)
Ask about the information kit on employer-assisted child care.
1509 16th Street N.W.
Washington, DC 20036-1426
(800) 424-2460

Child Care Aware
National Association of Child Care Resource and Referral Agencies
1319 F Street N.W., Suite 810
Washington, DC 20004
(800) 424-2246

The Fatherhood Project
c/o The Families and Work Institute
330 Seventh Avenue, Fourteenth Floor
New York, NY 10001
(212) 268-4846

School-Age Child Care Project
Center for Research on Women
Wellesley, MA 02181
(617) 283-2547

Children's Defense Fund
25 E Street N.W.
Washington, DC 20001

Child Care Action Campaign
330 Seventh Avenue, Seventeenth Floor
New York, NY 10001-5010
(212) 239-0138

National Association for Family Child Care
1331–A Pennsylvania Avenue, Suite 348
Washington, DC 20004
(800) 359-3817

International Nanny Association
125 S. Fourth Street
Norfolk, NE 68701
(402) 691-9628

AuPair in America
102 Greenwich Avenue
Greenwich, CT 06830
(800) 9AU-PAIR

Child Custody

Committee for Mother and Child Rights, Inc.
Support for mothers with custody problems related to divorce or contested custody
Route 1, Box 256A
Clearbrook, VA 22624
(703) 722-3652

Mothers Without Custody
P.O. Box 27418
Houston, TX 77227-7418
(800) 457-6962

Joint Custody Association
10606 Wilkins Avenue
Los Angeles, CA 90024
(310) 475-5352

United Fathers of America
595 City Drive, Suite 202
Orange, CA
(714) 385-1002

Father Focus
5480 Wisconsin Avenue, Suite 226
Chevy Chase, MD 20815
(301) 589-1414

National Center on Women and Family Law, Inc.
Send a stamped, self-addressed envelope to:
799 Broadway, Room 402
New York, NY 10003

The Academy of Family Mediators
P.O. Box 10501
Eugene, OR 97440
(503) 345-1205

Child Support

National Child Support Advocacy Coalition (NCSAC)
P.O. Box 420
Hendersonville, TN 37077-0420

Association for Children for Enforcement of Support (ACES)
723 Phillips Avenue, Suite 216
Toledo, OH 43612
(419) 472-6609

Office of Child Support Enforcement Administration for Children and Families
370 L'Enfant Promenade S.W., Fourth Floor
Washington, DC 20447

Organization for the Enforcement of Child Support
119 Nicodemus Road
Reisterstown, MD 21136

Financial Resources
Budgeting and Organizing

Consumer Credit Counseling (nonprofit), Education Department
(714) 544-8880
Ask for free booklets *Beating Budget Phobia, Budgeting and Planning: Building a Better Future,* and *Surviving and Controlling Debt.*

Certified Financial Planners
(800) 282-PLAN
Ask about their free pamphlet *How to Manage Your Financial Resources: Creating a Spending Plan You Can Control.*

Founders Funds of Denver
(800) 525-2440
Ask for their free personal financial organizer to keep track of your important papers and investments.

Children and Investing

Liberty Financial Companies Inc.
(800) 403-KIDS
Ask for the free *Liberty Financial Young Investor Parent Guide.*

Founders Funds of Denver
(800) 525-2440
Ask for the free booklet *The Gift of a Lifetime,* which explains the Uniform Gift to Minors Act and the Uniform Transfer to Minors Act.

College Planning

T. Rowe Price
(800) 638-5660
Ask for the free *College Planning Kit.*

Dreyfus Service Corp.
(800) 782-6620
Ask for the free *Guide to Investing for College.*

Fidelity Investments
(800) 544-6666
Ask for the free *College Savings Worksheet.*

The Institute of Certified Financial Planners
(800) 282-PLAN
Ask for the free booklet *Your Children's College Bill: How to Figure It . . . How to Pay for It.*

Credit Information

To review your total credit history, call the following agencies for a copy of your credit report. Contact all three agencies. Each may have different information on file.

TRW Consumer Assistance Center
P.O. Box 2350
Chatsworth, CA 91313-2350
(800) 392-1122

Equifax Information Service Center
P.O. Box 740241
Atlanta, GA 30375
(800) 685-1111

Trans Union Corporation
P.O. Box 7000
North Olmstead, OH 44070
(216) 779-2378

Additional help:

Federal Trade Commission
Ask about the brochures *Women & Credit Histories* and *Fair Credit Reporting*
Washington, DC 20580
(202) 326-2222

Estate Planning

Estate Planning for Divorced Parents
5820 Stoneridge Mall Road, Suite 100W
Pleasanton, CA 94588-3275
(510) 462-8483

Health

National Immunization Information Hotline
(800) 232-2522; (800) 232-0233 (Spanish)

Internet/Online Help

Sole Mothers International
http://home.navisoft.com/solemom

Single Parents Association
http://trojan.neta.com/~spa/

Parent Soup
http://www.parentsoup.com/

Pediatric Points of Interest
http://www.med.jhu.edu/peds/neonatology/poi2.htm/#Parenting

Single Parenting in the 90s
http://www.parentsplace.com/readroom/spn/spn_ord.html

Parenthood and Singlehood
http://www.xensei.com/users/ileneh/parent.html

Parents Helping Parents
http://www.portal.com/~cbntmkr/php.html

Positive Parenting
http://www.fishnet/~pparents

Smart Parenting
http://www.garlic.com/parents/

National Parents Information Network
http://ericps.edu.uiuc.edu/npin/npinhome.html

Estate Planning for Divorced Parents
http://www.ca-probate.com/a_divpar.htm

Federal Office of Child Support Enforcement
http://www.acf.dhhs.gov/programs/CSE/index.html

Bureau of Labor Statistics Occupational Handbook
gopher://gopher.umsl.edu/11/library/govdocs/ooha/oohb

U.S. Department of Education Student Aid web site
gopher://www.ed.gov: 80/hGET%20/prog-info/SFA/StudentGuide/1996-7/index.htm

Consumer Credit Counseling Service
http://www.Powersource.com/cccs/

Single Rose
http://home.aol.com/SINGLEROS1

WidowNet
http://www.fortnet.org/~goshorn/

Father's Rights & Equality Exchange
http://www.vix.com/free/

National Fatherhood Initiative
http://www.register.com/father/

Single Dad's Index
http://www.vix.com/men/single-dad.html

Organizations/Support Groups

Sole Mothers International
Diane Chambers, Director
P.O. Box 450246
Atlanta, GA 31145-0246
(770) 736-8601
Web site: http://home.navisoft.com/solemom

National Organization of Single Mothers
Andrea Engber, Director
P.O. Box 68
Midland, NC 28107-0068

Divorced and Widowed Women's Network
De Bargas Mall, Suite G455
Santa Fe, NM 87501

Parents Without Partners
National organization of divorced and widowed parents, with more than 650
local chapters all over the United States
8807 Colesville Road
Silver Spring, MD 20910
(800) 637-7974

Single Mothers By Choice
P.O. Box 1642
Gracie Square Station
New York, NY 10028
(212) 988-0993

Single Parent Resource Center
1165 Broadway
New York, NY 10001
(212) 947-0221

Sisterhood of Black Single Mothers, Inc.
1360 Fulton Street, Room 413
Brooklyn, NY 11216
(718) 638-0413

National Men's Resource Center
P.O. Box 800-PR
San Anselmo, CA 94979
(415) 453-2389

Widowed Persons Service
AARP
1901 K Street N.W.
Washington, DC 20049
(202) 872-4700

The Nurturing Network
For single pregnant women who wish to give birth, this organization can provide temporary housing, counseling, and other practical help.
(800) 866-4MOM

Banana Splits
A national group with many in-school chapters designed to help children cope with divorce. For more information, write:
Interactive Publishing Company
Box 997
Lakeside, CA 92040

Divorced Parent's X-change
P.O. Box 1127
Athens, OH 45701-1127

Periodicals

SMI Reporter
Official quarterly newsletter of Sole Mothers International
Subscription price: free
P.O. Box 450246
Atlanta, GA 31145-0246
(770) 736-8601

Single Parent Family
Full-color magazine published monthly by Focus on the Family
Suggested donation: $15 per year
8605 Explorer Drive
Colorado Springs, CO 80920-1051
(719) 531-5181

Full-Time Dads
P.O. Box 577
Cumberland, ME 04021
(207) 829-5260

The Single Parent
Publication of Parents Without Partners
401 North Michigan Avenue
Chicago, IL 60611
(312) 644-6610

SingleMOTHER
Publication of the National Organization of Single Mothers
P.O. Box 68
Midland, NC 28107-0068
(704) 888-KIDS

Welfare Mothers Voice
Subscription price: $15 per year
4504 N. Forty-Seventh Street
Milwaukee, WI 53218
(414) 444-0220

Single Rose
Monthly newsletter for single mothers
Subscription price: $12 per year
P.O. Box 487
Kennedale, TX 76060